The
SHETLAND
GUIDE BOOK

by Charles Tait

"Dispecta est et Thule" - Tacitus

ISBN 09517859 4 X

The Shetland Guide Book second edition
© copyright Charles Tait Photographic Ltd 2007
Published by Charles Tait Photographic Ltd
Kelton, St Ola, Orkney KW15 1TR
Tel 01856 873738 Fax 01856 875313

charles.tait@zetnet.co.uk   www.charles-tait.co.uk

This book is dedicated to my wife, Sandra.

Text, design and layout and all photographs © copyright Charles Tait unless otherwise credited. OS maps reproduced by permission of Ordnance Survey on behalf of The Controller of Her Majesty's Stationery Office. © Crown Copyright 100035677
Thanks to my assistant, Muriel, for cover concept and editorial input, Magnus for image processing and all in Shetland who have helped with this publication.
Printing by Kina Italia

ISBN 09517859 4 X

the SHETLAND GUIDE BOOK

by Charles Tait

hjaltland

CONTENTS

WELCOME TO SHETLAND

Jarlshof at Sumburgh has Bronze Age, Iron Age, Norse and later buildings in a complex and interesting site

Shetland is a chain of over 100 islands to the north east of Scotland which stretches nearly 90 miles (150km) from **Muckle Flugga** in the north (60°51'N, 0°53'W) to **Fair Isle** (59°31'N, 01°39'W) in the south. Sumburgh Head is 90 miles (150km) from Caithness in Scotland, and about 210 miles (340km) from Aberdeen. The Faeroes and Bergen are almost equidistant from Lerwick at about 250 miles (400km). The total land area is about 567 miles² (1,468km²), while the coastline exceeds 900 miles (1,500km).

The islands were referred to by Vikings as **Hjaltland**, possibly because of their resemblance to a sword handle (ON *hjalt*), but the name may also refer to the earlier inhabitants, referred to as the Catts by the Picts, who called Shetland *Innse Catt*, or Islands of the Catts. Today the Viking influence remains strong, as most place names and many local expressions derive from Old Norse (ON). About 22,000 people inhabit 13 of the islands, with the majority of the population living on the Mainland. The main town and ferry port is Lerwick with a population of about 8,000.

From Orkney on a clear day Shetland appears as a series of hilltops on the horizon (Foula, Fitful Head and Fair Isle), and when approached from the sea they at first seem rocky and bleak, but on closer approach the landscape turns out to be much gentler than expected, with characteristic greens, blues and browns of land, sea and coast.

It is likely that Pytheas the Greek may have visited Shetland about 325BC during his voyage around Britain during which he established a latitude of 60°, perhaps at Lerwick. Tacitus also refers to *"Thule"*, which was *"closely examined"* by the Romans when Agricola's fleet circumnavigated Britain in AD83 after the victory at *Mons Graupius*.

Shetland ponies

There are many references to the islands in the Norse sagas, which date from the 13th century, and a few documents still exist going back to late Norse times, which shed interesting light on the social history of the area.

It was not until the 18th century, however, that detailed accounts began to be made about visits to the islands. In more recent times many eminent people have visited Shetland and a number have written in various terms about their experiences.

Over the years many local authors have written about their homeland, and the Shetland Times Bookshop always has a large selection of local books. The library in Lerwick has a good reference section for those wishing to consult the many books which are "out of print". Shetland Museum has a large collection of old photographs, many of which may be seen on their website, while Shetland Archives is the place to research old documents.

Whether you want to read about archaeology, birds, fauna, landscapes or culture, I hope you will find my book to be a valuable

Atlantic Puffins, or "Tammy Nories" are one of the symbols of Shetland

point of reference and, from there, help you to enjoy, as I have, this savagely beautiful northern archipelago.

The people of Shetland,you will find to be friendly, hospitable and proud of their heritage yet, they are also very independent ,industrious and pro-active.

Before you start exploring I would recommend a visit to the Shetland Times Bookshop and the VisitShetland Tourist Centre (both in Lerwick) to source maps and other relevant literature. While some of the places mentioned in this book are signposted, most are not, and Ordnance Survey references are thus given for many sites of interest.

COUNTRYSIDE CODE

We are justly proud of our historic sites, wildlife and environment. Please help ensure that future visitors may enjoy them as much as you by observing these guidelines:

1. Always use stiles and gates and close gates after you.
2. Always ask permission before entering agricultural land.
3. Keep to paths and take care to avoid fields of grass and crops.
4. Do not disturb livestock.
5. Take your litter away with you and do not light fires.
6. Do not pollute water courses or supplies.
7. Never disturb nesting birds.
8. Do not pick wild flowers or dig up plants.
9. Drive and park with due care and attention - do not obstruct or endanger others.
10. Always take care near cliffs and beaches - particularly with children and pets. Many beaches are dangerous for swimmers.
11. Walkers should take adequate clothes, wear suitable footwear and tell someone of their plans.
12. Above all please respect the life of the countryside - leave only footprints, take only photographs and pleasant memories.

Notice: While some of the sites of interest are open to the public and have marked access, many are on private land. No right of access is implied in the description, and if in doubt it is always polite to ask. Also, while many roads and tracks are rights of way, not all are.

Lerwick Up Helly Aa takes place on the last Tuesday in January each year

Shetland has a wealth of archaeological and historical sites to visit. A few such as Mousa, Clickimin or Jarlshof are "official" monuments, while some others are signposted, but most are not. One of the real pleasures of Shetland is discovering ancient landscapes and structures for oneself.

The first settlers arrived around 4000BC, and they and those who followed left much behind them - many ruined houses, chambered cairns and field walls as well as numerous artefacts and burials. Neolithic, Bronze Age, Iron Age, Pictish, Norse, Medieval and later sites are dispersed all over the islands.

Apart from the large Neolithic hall at Stanydale, all of the chambered cairns and prehistoric houses are quite small and ruinous. However, their context in the landscape is uniquely visible on close observation.

There are *"burnt mounds"* dating from the Bronze Age all over the islands. Fire-heated stones were used to boil water in a central trough and thus cook meat.

Jarlshof has long been considered the most interesting of all Shetland's ancient monuments, having been continuously occupied for perhaps 4,000 years, but nearby Old Scatness now vies for that title. Continuing excavations there are casting much light on Iron Age Shetland.

Mousa Broch is the best preserved of over 100 such structures scattered all over Shetland, some of which still stand up to

Scord of Brouster settlement, Walls, West Mainland

Islesburgh chambered cairn, Northmavine

Jarlshof, Sumburgh - Bronze Age houses in foreground

Old Scatness, Sumburgh - Iron Age house

two metres high, and many of which are in splendid locations.

Wheelhouses such as may be seen at Jarlshof, Old Scatness and Clickimin were developed after the brochs were built.

Although a number of *"Pictish"* cross slabs and other artefacts have been found, no Pictish houses are on view. There are also remarkably few Norse buildings, apart from those at Jarlshof, and on Unst. There are many *"Norse"* mills distributed all over the islands which, however, date from more recent times.

Shetland has many early Christian sites, the most famous of which is St Ninian's Isle where the famous Pictish silver hoard was found. There are ruined chapels all over the islands, but none remains intact.

The 17th century "castles" at Scalloway and Muness are the result of the short-lived but pivotal Stewart era, while Fort Charlotte in Lerwick dates from the later 17th century, and many "laird's houses" were built in the 18th and 19th centuries.

Remains of the fishing industry ranging from Hanseatic and Dutch times to the 19th century *Haaf* fishing stations and later Herring Boom times are also scattered throughout the islands.

Artefacts from the 20th century, such as old gun emplacements, airbases, and memories of the *"Shetland Bus"*, as well as the current fishing and oil industries complete the varied picture.

"Blockhouse" at Ness of Burgi, Sumburgh

Mousa Broch from the south

Scalloway Castle

Fort Charlotte, Lerwick

NATURE AND ENVIRONMENT

The environment of Shetland is the result of its geology and climate, combined with the effects of glaciation, plants and animals, including man, over time. The *"Auld Rock"* as it is so affectionately known to islanders, is well named, as the underlying rocks are ancient gneisses and schists up to 3,000 million years old, which are mostly overlain by newer limestones, sandstones or volcanic intrusions.

St Ninian's Isle and ayre from Bigton, South Mainland

The waters around Shetland are nearly 100m deep within a short distance of the coastline in most places, and the land rises steeply from the continental shelf. Most of the terrestrial surface is, even by geological standards, very old indeed. Shetland today represents the remnants of an ancient mountain range worn down to its roots, which were at one time buried deep within the Earth.

Muckle Flugga from Hermaness, Unst

Several types of landscape occur in Shetland. These include moorland and hills, which cover most of the interior, often studded with lochs, fertile agricultural land in a few places where the rocks are favourable, coastal marshes, sandy beaches and dunes, rocky coasts and often high cliffs, long voes or sea lochs, small islands and skerries and sheltered bays and harbours.

Traditional hay-making, West Sandwick, Yell

Lochs of Kirkigarth and Bardister, Walls, West Mainland

A common coastal feature is the ayre (ON *Eyrr* - gravel beach) which is typically a gravelly spit, often covered with sand, which joins a small island to the Mainland, or which encloses a bay. Perhaps the best known is the tombolo leading to St Ninian's Isle, but there are many others.

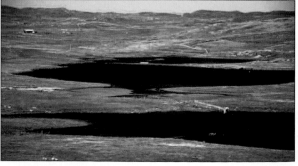

The voes are drowned valleys which were sculpted by glaciers. Shetland had a relatively thin ice cap in the last Ice Age, and the islands were ice free before mainland Scotland. The huge weight of ice on adjacent Scotland and Norway caused the land to fall and the sea bed to rise, but since the ice melted, the sea bed has sunk and sea level has risen, as have the larger land areas. As a result substantial areas which were above sea level 10,000 years ago are now submerged.

winter sunset over Whiteness Voe from Wormadale

The relatively mild, but windy and damp oceanic climate, is controlled by the North Atlantic weather systems with their procession of depressions giving wind, rain and fine weather, but when a Scandinavian high pressure extends over Shetland, fine weather may be enjoyed for weeks at a time.

Peat bank above Ronas Voe, North Mainland

The temperature of the sea ranges from a minimum of about 6^0 in February to a maximum of about 12^0 in August, ensuring that summers are cool and damp, and winters are mild. The warmest month is August (mean max 16^0) and the coldest February (mean min 3^0). The sunniest months are May and June, while the darkest is December. The driest months are April, May and June, while the wettest tend to be October, November, December and January.

Sumburgh and Pool of Virkie with Exnaboe in foreground, Dunrossness

Chambered cairn on summit of Ronas Hill, Northmavine (450m)

Even in the depths of winter there are always fine *"days atween wadders"* and the variable climate also ensures an environment with ever changing light - paradise for artists and photographers!

Atlantic Puffin - Tammy Norie

Shetland is justly famous for its wildlife, and especially for birds. Over 1 million seabirds comprising 21 species (excluding divers, seaducks and phalaropes) breed every summer along the coasts and on the moors and lochs of the archipelago. Many of these spectacular colonies are accessible from land or water, especially those at Sumburgh, Noss and Hermaness.

Apart from the main breeding sites listed opposite, the various ferry crossings between and to the islands often afford excellent viewing opportunities, for seabirds as well as for cetaceans and seals. In particular the trips to Mousa, Fair Isle, Skerries and Foula often yield good sightings.

The seabirds are attracted to Shetland waters to breed for the same reason that fishermen have found the area so bountiful over the centuries. The Atlantic Slope Current flows north east along the edge of the continental shelf, where its relatively warmer, more saline water mixes with the water of the continental shelf itself, causing an upwelling of nutrients and warmth. This promotes the growth of phytoplankton in the long northern summer, which in turn feed zooplankton, cetaceans, small fish, bigger fish and of course birds.

There are huge Gannet colonies at Noss and Hermaness and smaller ones on Foula and Fair Isle. These spectacular birds may be seen diving at many locations as well, especially at Noss. The comical and popular Puffin as well as other auks may also be observed at very close quarters in several places. Large numbers of the aggressive Great Skua, along with some of the more graceful Arctic Skua breed on Hermaness and Foula.

Although less numerous than previously, the Arctic Tern remains the ubiquitous sign of summer in the islands. Along with a small number of Common Tern, these attractive birds may be seen fishing all around the coast.

Other common species include Gulls, Eider, Shag and Cormorant, but their numbers are

Great Skua - Bonxie

Gannets - Solan or Sula

Storm Petrel - Mootie

dwarfed by the Fulmar Petrel, of which about 300,000 breed on the coast and inland. Storm Petrel nest in large numbers in the stonework of Mousa Broch, while a few of the rare Leach's Petrel nest on Foula.

The "seabird cities", a hive of

Arctic Tern - Tirrick

activity in the breeding season, are mostly deserted once the young are fledged. Terns head for southern latitudes, while auks and petrels go offshore in search of food and safety from predators.

Seabird populations are in a con-

tinual state of fluctuation, and in recent years some species have grown in numbers and distribution (Gannet, Fulmar, Great Skua, Guillemot), while others have declined (Terns, Kittiwake). Reasons include exploitation or persecution by man and alterations in food supply whether by over-fishing, changes in climate or ocean currents or expansion of other competing species.

Many birds are sensitive to man-made environmental threats such as oil pollution or discharges of harmful chemicals. Exceptionally bad weather, whether in winter or during critical parts of the breeding season, or food shortages due to poor growing seasons also play a large part in these fluctuations.

Guillemot - Loom or Lungi

Fulmar Petrel - Maalie

Leach's Petrel

BREEDING SEABIRDS IN SHETLAND
Numbers in estimated pairs

Fulmar Petrel (300,000)
Storm Petrel (4,000)
Leach's Petrel (20?)
Manx Shearwater (10?)
Black Guillemot (7,500)
Guillemot (90,000)
Razorbill (6,500)
Puffin (100,000)
Greater Black-backed Gull (2,500)
Herring Gull (4,000)
Lesser Black-backed Gull (500)
Common Gull (2,500)
Black-headed Gull (<250)
Kittiwake (36,000)
Arctic Tern (10,000)
Common Tern (500)
Gannet (21,000)
Cormorant (<250)
Shag (6,000)
Great Skua (6,000)
Arctic Skua (2,000)
Eider Duck (7,000)

WHERE TO SEE BREEDING SEABIRDS
Mainland - Sumburgh Head, Fitful Head, No Ness, Skelda Ness, Eshaness, Uyea
Islands - Fair Isle, Mousa, Noss (Nature Reserve), Hermaness (Unst) (Nature Reserve), Burravoe (Yell), Fetlar, Papa Stour, Foula, Vaila.

Eider Duck - Dunter

Nature and Environment

Red-throated Diver - Rain Gjus

Wheatear - Stinkle

The Shetland landscape with its mix of croftland, "improved" farmland, moors, lochs, sheltered voes, small areas of woodland and varied coastline offers an attractive environment to about 50 land and water birds for breeding. There are also a number of irregular breeders, as well as some species which no longer breed here, but which may again in future.

Changes in land use, variations in climate and supply of suitable prey are all factors which influence breeding. While the number of species may be small the selection is special, and opportunities to observe them are excellent. In summer the Shetland landscape comes alive with birds. Breeding passerines include Twite, Wheatear, Rock and

Meadow Pipits, Skylark and two subspecies of Wren. Starlings are very common around the crofts, while Blackbirds nest in small numbers. Several other species occasionally breed including Reed Bunting and White Wagtail.

Twite - Lintie

Of the 13 species of waders, Whimbrel are locally common, and a small number of Red-necked Phalarope breed on Fetlar. Others include the Oystercatcher, Ringed and

Golden Plovers as well as Curlew, Lapwing, Redshank, Snipe and Dunlin.

Corncrake, Quail and Corn Bunting have all ceased breeding, no doubt due to changes in haymaking and modern agricultural practice. The rasp of the Corncrake used to be the sound of summer, but is no longer heard in Shetland. As traditional forms of land use disappear, so unfortunately may species which depend upon them.

Oystercatcher - Shalder

Ringed Plover - Sandy-loo

Golden Plover - Plivver

Red-necked Phalarope - Peerie Deuk

Whimbrel - Peerie or Tang Whaap

Red-throated Divers breed on many of the lochs and may often be seen or heard flying over on their way to and from their feeding grounds. They may also be observed from the car on small lochs, but care should be taken not to disturb them.

Apart from Mallard and Teal, ducks only breed in small numbers, including Wigeon, Shoveler and Tufted Duck. A few Mute Swans have bred in recent years and Whooper Swans have also recently bred successfully. Eider Ducks are common around the voes, while Red-breasted Mergansers breed beside freshwater lochs, but otherwise are mostly on the sea and shore. A small number of Shelduck also breed, mostly around the Pool of Virkie.

The only raptor to breed at present is the Merlin, which is recovering after a population crash in the 1980s. The Peregrine ceased breeding in the 1990s, most likely due to harassment by Fulmars, whose oil damages other birds' feathers, which may also be preventing the return of the White-tailed Sea Eagle.

The deep croak of the Raven is often heard, and they are frequently seen over the moors and along the coast. They nest early and their display flight can enliven many a dreich early spring day. Rock Doves are also common, and seem to have coped with Fulmars by nesting in places such as caves which the latter do not use. They may also have benefited from the demise of the Peregrine.

Merlin - Peerie Hawk

Red-breasted Merganser - Herald

Raven - Corbie or Rafn

LAND & WATER BIRDS TO SEE IN SHETLAND

Great Northern Diver
Red-throated Diver
Red-necked Phalarope
Dunlin
Oystercatcher
Curlew
Whimbrel
Merlin
Ringed Plover
Golden Plover
Lapwing
Twite
Wheatear
Meadow Pipit
Rock Pipit
Skylark
Wren
Rock Dove
Red-breasted Merganser
Shelduck
Raven

Great Northern Diver - Immer Goose

Robin

MIGRANTS Many species of birds have evolved life cycles whereby they travel north to breed, taking advantage of the brief but bounteous summer to feed their young, and then return south to winter in Britain, Europe or Africa.

The Northern Isles lie in the normal track of migrants returning south from Greenland, Iceland, Spitzbergen and Scandinavia. Additionally many species breeding further east (or west) may, because of adverse weather systems, unusual wind directions, or fog, end up further west (or east) than their normal routes.

Fair Isle, with its Bird Observatory, is a Mecca for bird watchers, and is a prime location for those wishing to observe migrants. To date 359 species have been recorded there, of which only about 45 are regular or occasional breeders.

Shetland as a whole is a stepping stone for migrants, and rare or unexpected species may turn up almost anywhere. The eastern outlying islands and the southern part of the Mainland are, however, the "hotspots" normally.

The spring migration begins in March with the return of waders and a few passerines, and about the start of April the breeding seabird species are returning. spring takes a while to appear in Shetland, and April is normally still quite cold, so that it is not until May that the main passage of common migrants, as well as falls of unusual numbers of regular species, or appearances of vagrants, take place.

The weather is the governing factor, and its unpredictable

Snow Bunting - Sna Fool

nature only adds to the excitement and anticipation for keen birders.

Waders start to pass through by the end of July, and through August migrants steadily increase, reaching a peak by the

Long-tailed Duck - Caaloo

Whooper Swan

end of the month. It is, however, September that is the peak month for rarities as well as several uncommon, but regular visitors. Depending on the weather, early October can also be a very good time for birders.

WINTER VISITORS

Although only a few species spend the winter in Shetland, they are interesting all the same. Goldeneye, Mallard, Wigeon, Teal and Whooper Swans frequent the lochs, while Eider, Slavonian Grebe, Great Northern Diver, Red-breasted Merganser, Goosander, Common Scoter, Scaup and Long-tailed Duck are seen in the voes and bays.

Waders including Turnstone, Redshank, Purple Sandpiper, Curlew, Lapwing, Golden Plover and Ringed Plover frequent tidal areas, especially at the heads of voes and sheltered shallow bays. Interestingly, only a few Oystercatchers overwinter in Shetland.

Small numbers of Long-eared Owl regularly overwinter, while Ring-billed, Glaucous and Iceland Gulls, Little Auk and Snow Bunting are are also often seen. Arctic species like King Eider, White-billed Diver,

Red-backed Shrike

Long-eared Owl - Catyogle

Gyrfalcon, Ross's and Ivory Gulls also may be seen occasionally.

Thus Shetland has something for the birder during almost every month of the year. Whether rare vagrants in migration times, breeding seabirds in summer, or wintering Arctic breeders, there is always something to see.

Redwing

MIGRATION TIMES

From mid-March to early June - May/start June best
From end July to early October - September best

COMMON MIGRANTS

Snow Bunting
Wheatear
Robin
Great Northern Diver
Long-tailed Duck
Bluethroat
Redwing
Fieldfare
Geese
Whooper Swan
Swallow
Long-eared Owl

BEST MIGRANT SITES

Islands - Fair Isle
Fetlar, Skerries & Whalsay
Foula & Mousa
Mainland - Sumburgh,
Scatness, Pool of Virkie,
Spiggie Loch, Loch of
Brue, Loch of Hillwell
Lerwick & Scalloway
Harbours, Tingwall Loch,
Whiteness, Tresta,
Kergord, Watsness, Voe,
Vidlin, Sullom Voe

Sanderling

Edmondston's Mouse-ear Chickweed on Keen of Hamar, Unst

MOORLAND About 50% of Shetland is covered with a blanket of peat, in places many feet thick, which has formed over the last few thousand years. Such areas are mostly wet and deficient in nutrients, and thus only support a limited range of plants. These include Cotton Grass, Bog Asphodel, Milkwort and Tormentil.

The Sundew and Butterwort are insectivorous, and trap small flies on their leaves. In late summer the moors take on a beautiful mauve tint when the Heather blooms. In moorland areas where conditions allow soils to be more free-draining, different plants thrive depending on the underlying rocks, as well as the degree of grazing. In particular the limestone areas are very noticeable by their relative "green-ness". These rich grassy areas can have an especially diverse range of plants.

Soon after the end of the last Ice Age, about 10,000 years ago, plants started to recolonise Shetland. The present vegetation of the islands is the result of the interactions between the roughly 400 successful species, the underlying, mostly acidic rocks, the climate and latitude and, for the last 5,000 years, the impact of man and his grazing animals.

Initial impressions are of very extensive peaty moorland stretching from one end of Shetland to the other. However, a closer look soon reveals a diversity of plant life, and between May and August a variety of habitats put on a rich floral display.

FELLFIELD The high granite areas of the North Mainland, such as Ronas Hill, and the serpentinite areas of Unst have remained as *fellfield*, where vegetation is sparse, and much bare rock, broken by frost action, is exposed. The plants which do survive are arctic or dwarf varieties, of which there are 15 on Ronas Hill.

The **Keen of Hamar**, on Unst, is the largest of several such areas on Unst and Fetlar and is home to the unique **Edmondston's Mouse-ear Chickweed**, along with several other species which have adapted to the inhospitable conditions.

CROFTLAND The old agricultural practices did much to encourage wildlife. Formerly many more cattle than sheep were kept, and they needed large quantities of winter feed. This was provided by hay meadows, which were only grazed early and late in the season, and were cut in August. Cattle dung is

Hard Fern on Ronas Hill

Fir Clubmoss on Ronas Hill

Milkwort, Keen of Hamar, Unst

Heather

spring Squill

also not acidic, unlike sheep droppings.

Sheep have largely replaced cattle, except on the small number of larger farms, but there are still many old meadows, field boundaries, verges, burns, steep slopes and other places where the Shetland sheep does not reach. These are havens for many species of wild flower including, in early summer, spring Squill and Primrose *(Mayflower)*, followed by Orchids, Buttercups, Hawkbits, Clovers, Field Gentian, Eyebright, Vetches and a wide range of grasses.

Damper areas which have remained undrained may have Irises, Heath Spotted Orchid, Ragged Robin, Marsh Marigold and Cotton Grass.

Thrift

Eyebright

Orchid, Keen of Hamar, Unst

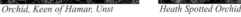

Heath Spotted Orchid

Primrose

Cotton Grass

Ladies Bedstraw

COASTLINE Nowhere in Shetland is more than 3 miles from the sea so in many ways the whole area is "coastal" in that it is all affected by salt in the air to some degree. The roughly 900 miles of coast include many habitats for plants. These include exposed shores and cliffs, sheltered bays and voes, salt marshes, sandy beaches and dunes and maritime heath.

Lichens thrive even in the most exposed of locations, especially the yellow *Xanthoria* and hairy *Ramalina ("Old Man's Beard")* which are so prominent, and benefit from the clean air and water.

In summer plants such as Thrift, spring Squill, Plantains and short grasses, give colour to the clifftops, while species like Sea Rocket, Scurvy Grass, Oysterplant and Silverweed grow on more sheltered beaches. Sea Campion, Scentless Mayweed, Kidney Vetch, Vetches, Iris and Orchids often grow slightly inland, especially where protected from grazing.

Shetland does not have the extensive machair areas of the Western Isles, but the beaches with sand dune systems at Sumburgh, Quendale, Spiggie, St Ninian's Isle, West Sandwick and Breakon in Yell and Norwick and Skaw in Unst are the best examples. All are full of wildflowers in summer, especially the ungrazed areas.

Apart from those which are inhabited, there are over 80 small islands ranging from large holms such as Hascosay or Balta to isolated skerries such as the Ve Skerries or the Ramna Stacks. Depending on the rock type, degree of exposure and whether or not there are sheep or nesting birds present, these islands have a varying range of flora. Some are very lush, while others are so

Sheep's Bit Scabious

exposed as to have virtually no plants at all.

In most parts of Shetland the shore is steep to, and not gently shelving as in Orkney. As a result of this and the limited tidal range, most beaches only have a narrow intertidal littoral zone. Shetland thus mostly lacks the extensive seaweed resources of Orkney or the Western Isles, which have had such a beneficial effect on farmland in these areas.

Sea Plantain

Ramalina covers many old buildings

Thrift thrives in coastal areas

Xanthoria adds colour

Scentless Mayweed

Water Lilies grow on some of the lochs

LOCHS AND MARSHES

There may only be a few large lochs in Shetland, but there are hundreds of small ones, ranging from little pools and marshy areas to "proper" lochs. There are no large streams, but many lesser ones, several of which drain into areas of salt marsh at the head of voes. Small holms on many of the lochs, as well as inaccessible burnsides and craigs provide protection from grazing and in the latter cases shelter.

There are restricted areas of relict "woodland" in these localities, showing that some trees and shrubs can grow in Shetland. The range of plants in these places probably reflects the sort of vegetation which covered much of Shetland before the arrival of

man and his grazing animals. This is confirmed by studies of pollen grains taken from cores of loch sediments.

Many of the more acid lochs have Water Lilies, which provide a contrast to the browns and purples of the surrounding moorland. More nutrient-rich lochs often have Marsh Marigolds, Iris and Ragged Robin along their shores.

Kidney Vetch

Marsh Marigold

Silverweed

Sea Rocket

Scurvy Grass

Oyster Plant

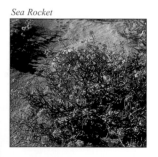

Laurie Campbell

Otters frequent many of the shores in suitable locations - Draatsi

Otter tracks are often seen

All of the land mammals in Shetland have been introduced by man. Otters are now thought to have arrived perhaps with early Norse settlers, along with Field and House Mice, while all of the others apart from the ubiquitous Brown Rat are much more recent.

The **Otter** *(Draatsi)* is a coastal animal in Shetland and is quite common with perhaps 800 individuals. They prefer small uninhabited holms and sheltered rocky shores with abundant seaweed where they can catch their prey which mostly consists of Eelpout, Butterfish and Rockling.

Although they feed in the sea, the Otter's coat is not adapted to sea water, and it must come ashore frequently to wash and dry its coat to avoid becoming waterlogged and chilled. Holts are virtually always near a stream or small loch, and usually within a mile of the sea, so that where streams outflow to suitable shorelines tend to be good places to look for Otters. Either early morning or late evening tends to be the best time of day to see this elusive animal. Patience and perseverance will eventually repay the observer!

Both **Grey** *(Haaf Fish)* and **Common** or **Harbour** *(Tang Fish)* **Seals** or *Selkies* are rela-

tively common in Shetland, with populations of about 3,500 and 6,200 respectively. Common Seals have their pups in June, and may be seen all around sheltered coastlines. One of the largest colonies is on Mousa, where they may be quite closely observed without disturbance.

In contrast, Grey Seals have their pups in Autumn when they go ashore on small, uninhabited islands or remote beaches to give birth to and suckle their pups. Large numbers come ashore on the Lang Ayre, the spectacular but remote beach to the west of Ronas Hill, while even more pup on the inaccessible Ve Skerries.

Grey Seal pup

Grey Seal mother and pup - Haaf Fish

Cetaceans are regularly seen around the coasts. Most common are **Harbour Porpoise** *(Neesick)*, while **Atlantic White-sided**, **White-beaked** and **Risso's Dolphin** are also quite often seen off the east coast. **Killer Whales** regularly make appearances, and several pods appear to be semi-resident.

Humpback Whales are sometimes seen off Sumburgh Head

Large whales are observed regularly feeding on the edge of the continental shelf, and quite often come inshore, especially in summer, when they seem to find the waters around Sumburgh Head attractive. The most commonly seen is **Minke** *(Herring Hog)* which follows shoals of Mackerel and Herring, as does the **Humpback** which is seen regularly in this area.

Risso's Dolphin

Pilot *(Caa'in)* **Whales** are also regular coastal visitors, usually in small pods, while **Sperm Whales** appear to be becoming more common, but sadly usually as strandings of dead animals. The larger baleen whales are normally only seen offshore near the 1,000m line, which is only 60 nautical miles from the west of Shetland, where they feed on the abundant plankton resulting from the Atlantic Slope Current.

Minke Whale - Herring Hog

Common Seal - Tang Fish

SEA MAMMALS COMMONLY SEEN

Common Seal
Grey Seal
Killer Whale (Orca)
Humpback Whale
Minke Whale
Sperm Whale
Pilot Whale
Dolphins & Porpoises

MAMMALS INTRODUCED

Otter (pre-Norse)
Stoat (1600's ?)
Ferret (1980's)
Rabbit (unknown)
Blue Hare (early 1900's)
Hedgehog (1800's)
Brown Rat
Field Mouse (Vikings)
House Mouse (pre-Norse?)

Common Seals frequent sheltered shores and sea lochs

Eshaness

ARCHAEOLOGY AND HISTORY

Shetland Museum

The chambered cairn on Vementry has a well preserved facade and chamber

The first people to arrive in Shetland may possibly have been Mesolithic hunter-gatherers, before 5000BC. Although no direct evidence of such people has been found, perhaps because any traces may have been lost to the sea, pollen studies do suggest that there were changes in the vegetation around that time which may have been caused by man.

The oldest remaining structures are the large number of chambered cairns, houses and field walls left by Neolithic farmers. Excavations of the settlement at Scord of Brouster have revealed radiocarbon dates of 3250BC for the earliest stone house, which was built on top of an ear-

lier wooden one, while the oldest burial so far dated was a large stone cist at Sumburgh in which were bones representing at least 18 people dating from about 3200BC.

Chambered cairns were much the commonest form of burial in Neolithic times and at least 100 are scattered all over Shetland, often occupying prominent sites on the skyline and overlooking farm settlements. Many are very ruinous, having been used by later generations as quarries, which is not surprising given the hardness of the local stone.

Most of these cairns are described as *"heel-shaped"*, and are ovoid in shape with a curved

and well built facade in the middle of which is the entrance passage, leading into a semi-rectangular chamber, which would have had a corbelled roof covered with small stones. The cairns vary in size from quite small to extremely large (4 to 20 metres in diameter).

None of the better-preserved sites is particularly accessible. The little cairn at **Islesburgh** (HU693685), near Mavis Grind, is, however, both impressive and easy to reach. Other sites at **Muckle Ward** on Vementry (HU295609), **Punds Water**, Mangaster (HU325713) and **Ronas Hill**, Northmavine (HU305835), are harder to reach but well worth the effort.

Many such structures were dug into in the past, destroying any structure in the process. So far the few chambered cairns which have recently been excavated have been disappointing in that they have not yielded very much in the way of artefacts. Preservation of bone is not normally good in the Shetland environment and the generally ruinous condition of most of the cairns means that any useful evidence has long since gone.

Islesburgh heel-shaped chambered cairn

Islesburgh heel-shaped chambered cairn

Chambered cairn on Ronas Hill

Ronas Hill - interior

Even in their present state many of these sites remain very dramatic. These include the *"Giant's Stones"* at **Housetter**, Northmavine (HU362855) where all that remains are the monoliths which mark the ends of a once-impressive facade, together with a scatter of stones.

Several sites in spectacular situations are worth a visit as they overlook the landscape of the Neolithic farmers who built them. These include **Nesbister Hill** (HU402454), **Ward of Culswick** (HU263462), **March Cairn** (HU222788), **Ward of Scousburgh** (HU388188) and **Ward of Symbister** (HU533620). More suggestions are included in the area gazetteer.

"Giant's Stones", Housetter, Northmavine

Shetland Museum

Punds Water entrance passage

Sumburgh cist burial artefacts

NEOLITHIC AND BRONZE AGES TIMELINE

BC	
c.10000	Ice in retreat
c.6000	Woodland widespread, first hunter-gatherers arrive?
c.4000	First farmers?
3200	Oldest radiocarbon dates
3000	Chambered Cairns
2000	Chambered tombs sealed
1800	"Bronze Age" cist burials
1500	Climatic deterioration
1200	Burnt mounds
700	Bronze finally in use

CHAMBERED CAIRNS TO VISIT

MAINLAND

Ward of Scousburgh, South
Nesbister Hill, Whiteness
Park Hall, Bixter
Muckle Ward, Vementry
Cattapund Knowe, Walls
Gallow Hill, Walls
Seli Voe, West Mainland
Ward of Culswick, W Mainland
Islesburgh, Mavis Grind
Punds Water, Mangaster
March Cairn, Eshaness
Ronas Hill, Northmavine
Housetter, Northmavine
Islesburgh, Northmavine

ISLANDS

Pettigarth's Field, Whalsay
Ward of Symbister, Whalsay
Windhouse, Yell
Muckle Heog, Unst

Stanydale, West Mainland

There are ruins of at least 180 houses in Shetland dating from Neolithic to Iron Age times. Together with associated field walls, cairns and the results of excavations they present a remarkable picture of life then. The West Mainland is a good place to start looking, especially in areas where there is no thick layer of peat.

The houses are oval in shape, and up to 10 metres wide. The substantial stone walls have a rubble and earth core, and well-built facings. They are usually surrounded by walls which look like in-fields, out-fields and boundary dykes.

Inside there is a large hearth area in the middle which is usually rather lower than the rest of the house and often has drains leading outside. This is surrounded by several alcoves or cells , and normally the floor is paved with flat stones. The outside wall at the entrance is often curved in a similar manner to the facades of the chambered cairns and there is usually a porch.

In some cases there is evidence of post holes indicating roof supports. No doubt the roofs were constructed from wood or whalebone covered with heather and turf. Excavation has revealed that many of these sites were occupied for a long time, with houses being rebuilt on the same site. Many of these struc-

tures are buried in peat, and come to light during peat cutting. It seems that it was the encroachment of blanket peat which caused most of these houses and fields to be abandoned, perhaps as recently as the late Iron Age.

Typically the houses are found in small groups, near a water source, and usually in areas of good land. Frequently there are associated chambered cairns, and *"burnt mounds"*. The people kept cattle, and some sheep. They grew barley, and ploughed using stone-tipped ards.

In the absence of flint, quartz was used to make sharp tools, while both soapstone and fired clay were used to make pots. The acidic conditions do not allow bone or much other organic material to survive, except for pollen grains, whose analysis has yielded much information about the vegetation. The arrival of settlers is indicated by a reduction in woodland species, and an increase in plants typical of agricultural pasture, due to clearance by people and their grazing animals, followed ultimately by the development of peat over wide areas.

Pinhoulland, West Mainland

Scord of Brouster, Walls

Scord of Brouster, Walls

There is a particularly large structure at **Stanydale** (HU285502) which resembles the other oval houses, but is much bigger with interior dimensions of 7x12m and substantial walls up to 5m thick. The inside is faced with massive stones, some over 1m high, and overall the building is heel-shaped with a well-built convex facade at the entrance.

Neolithic pottery was found here, dating from perhaps 2500BC, but pottery of Iron Age type was also found, suggesting a long period of use. There were two large post-holes, one of which had the remains of two carbonised Spruce poles still in it, presumably the remains of roof-supports.

The walls have six large alcoves,

about 2.5 by 1.3m in size, built into them, which are divided by radial piers, each of which is faced by a large upright stone. The building may have had some function such as being the local "Community Hall" or "Church".

Shetland Museum

Punds Water, Mangaster

Shetland Museum

Quartz arrow heads

Neolithic pottery

Benie Hoose, Whalsay

SETTLEMENT SITES TO VISIT

MAINLAND

Clickimin, Lerwick
Dalseter, Boddam
Jarlshof, Sumburgh
Newing, South Nesting
Lunning, Lunnasting
Scord of Brouster, Walls
Pinhoulland, Walls
Stanydale, W Mainland
Gruting School, W Mainland
Punds Water, Mangaster

ISLANDS

Beorgs of Uyea, Unst
Benie Hoose, Whalsay
Yoxie Hoose, Whalsay

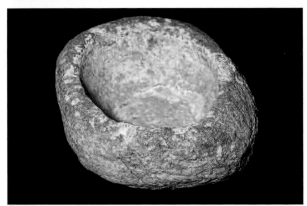

Steatite pot

The inhabitants of Shetland used stone to make objects and tools until quite recent times. The lack of wood and flint meant that the early settlers had to find alternatives. Conveniently there are several outcrops of steatite or soapstone (ON *kleberg* - loom weight), a soft rock, related to talc, which can be worked with stone or metal tools to make many objects, including pots, plates, weights for fishing or looms, and so on.

Soapstone becomes hard and strong when fired, as well as heat-resistant, and was used from the Neolithic to recent times. The extensive quarries at **Catpund** in Cunningsburgh on the South Mainland (HU426272) have much evidence of working of this convenient mineral.

Another unusual artefact found locally is the **"Shetland Knife"**. These flat stone knives, as well as axe-heads and other carved stone objects were made from felsite from the north of Unst at the **Beorgs of Uyea** (HU327900), the only such outcrop in Britain

Although polished stone artefacts were common in the Neolithic, these *"knives"* are unique to Shetland, and are made from thin sheets of rock, which have been skillfully polished and one edge sharpened. They are 15-20cm long and about 5mm thick, and seem to have been for show rather than actual use as knives. Much evidence of working and even a stone shelter can be seen at the Beorgs of Uyea.

Shetland knives have turned up in peat cuttings on several occasions, often far from any known prehistoric settlement site, and are sometimes carefully arranged, perhaps as votive offerings of some kind.

Although there are no stone circles or stone rows in Shetland, there are plenty of isolated standing stones, most of which are of indeterminate date. Some may be glacial erratics, while others have clearly been specially quarried and erected. Many have folk tales about them.

Standing stones may have been erected as sea marks, in memory of an important person or event, or for some religious reason. They may also have been erect-

Polished stone artefacts

Polished stone artefacts

Standing stone, Clivocast, Unst

Standing stone, Bordastubble, Unst

There are several enigmatic stone rings, or enclosures, which consist of small boulders which may be in a turf bank. The function of these monuments is not clear, although they might be Bronze Age cemeteries, where cremations were buried, or undertaken. Some may also be the remains of burial cairns.

The best example is **Hjaltadans** (HU618928) on Fetlar where 22 serpentine stones surround a low circular bank, at the centre of which are two larger stones. **Battle Pund** (HU684713) on Skerries, and the **Rounds of Tivla** (HP616107) on Unst may be similar sites.

ed as status symbols or as boundary markers. Some are also remaining parts of chambered cairns.

Battle Pund, Skerries

Felsite, Beorgs of Uyea

"Shetland Knives"

SITES TO VISIT

STEATITE QUARRIES

Catpund, Cunningsburgh
Fethaland, Northmavine
Clibberswick, Unst
Strandburgh, Fetlar
Valhammars, Fetlar

SHETLAND KNIVES

Shetland Museum, Lerwick
Beorgs of Uyea, Northmavine

STANDING STONES

Cruester, Bressay
Troswick, S Mainland
Yaa Field, East Burra
Mid Field, West Burra
Murder Stone, Tingwall
Lunning, Lunnasting
Skellister, South Nesting
Wester Skeld, W Mainland
Busta Voe, Brae
Hamnavoe, Eshaness

Lumbister, Yell
Bordastubble stone, Unst
Clivocast stone, Unst
Ripple stone, Fetlar

STONE ENCLOSURES

Battle Pund, Skerries
Hjaltadans, Fetlar
Rounds of Tivla, Unst
Stone Ring, Wormadale
Housa Voe, Papa Stour

Bronze Age houses at Jarlshof

The period from about 1800BC to 600BC is generally referred to as the "Bronze Age", and although bronze itself did not appear in Shetland until perhaps 700BC, some of the cultural aspects of this period did reach the islands, although it has been argued that culture in Shetland during this period was impoverished compared to Orkney.

During this time there was a steady deterioration in the climate, perhaps in part caused by eruptions of Icelandic volcanoes like Hekla, which resulted in the encroachment of peat further and further onto what had been good agricultural land, and the abandonment of settlements which had been occupied for

perhaps 2,000 years.

Throughout this period the people lived in houses very similar to those of the Neolithic, and good examples may be seen at Jarlshof and Clickimin. One innovation was the *"souterrain"*. These were small underground chambers accessed from within the house and were probably for food storage. There are several to be seen at Jarlshof.

During expansion of Sumburgh Airport in 1967 a prehistoric house was discovered and extensively investigated. This site turned out to have been occupied for a long time, from about 2000BC until abandoned perhaps 1,500 years later.

The site is now under the runway, and remains the only such site to have been recently excavated. The interior of the houses had recesses built into the walls similar to those on Whalsay and Jarlshof, and these seem to have been a standard feature of Shetland houses for a long time. Another interesting feature was that the entrance of the south house had a curved facade reminiscent of those on the earlier *"heel-shaped"* cairns.

While houses do not seem to have changed much during this period, the treatment of the dead did. During the Neolithic period inhumation was the normal practice, where bodies were buried whole, in chambered cairns, cists or in the ground, perhaps after exposure to allow the flesh to decompose, and normally in communal graves.

In contrast, during the Bronze Age, individual burial became the norm, often after cremation of the body. *"Beaker"* type pottery also appears at this time, and these vessels were frequently included in burials. These vase-like beakers were normally fine-

Trough in crescent of burnt mound, Burnside, Hillswick

Broken, burnt stones in mound at Crawton, Sandness

ly made with incised decoration, and appear in houses along with larger and less elegant *"urns"*. The latter were used as domestic containers as well as to bury cremated remains.

A further new development which also reached Shetland in the Bronze Age was the *"burnt mound"*, of which there are about 300 spread all through the islands. These crescent-shaped mounds are common throughout Britain and are normally situated near a source of fresh water and contemporary settlements. They consist of piles of burnt and shattered stone surrounding a central hearth and normally a large trough.

There are several theories about the function of these places, but it seems clear that the people used hot stones to boil water in the trough, most probably to cook meat. However, they may well also have served as bath houses, or saunas, and could have played a role in the dyeing and processing of cloth. It is unclear if any roofed structures were present.

So far no evidence of bronze working has been discovered in Shetland before about 700BC. About this date one of the houses at Jarlshof was used as a workshop for the casting of bronze objects, including axe heads, swords and jewellery. Quantities of clay moulds, crucibles, peat ash and charcoal were found on excavation. It is interesting that weapons were being manufactured at this time as they are generally unusual finds in Shetland.

The lack of bronze working in Shetland prior to this may be due to a lack of communication with the outside world. While there are several veins of copper ore on the Mainland and on Fair Isle, there is no evidence of ancient workings, and neither is there any source of tin.

Shetland Museum

Quartz arrowhead

Shetland Museum

Ard marks found under house

Jarlshof souterrain

Sumburgh houses under excavation

Shetland Museum

BRONZE AGE SITES TO VISIT

BURNT MOUNDS

Cruester, Bressay
Quendale, Sumburgh
Burraland, Walls
Crawton, Sandness
Burnside, Hillswick
Crosskirk, Eshaness

Kettlester, Yell
Houlalie, Pund, Fair Isle

HOUSES

Jarlshof
Clickimin
Scord of Brouster
Staneydale
Whalsay (Yoxie & Benie)

BRONZE WORKINGS

Jarlshof

ARCHAEOLOGY AND HISTORY

Burland Broch, Brindister

The start of the Iron Age around 500BC marks a big change to life in Shetland. Along with iron tools came the sudden development of brochs, blockhouses and wheelhouses. This reflects similar developments especially in Orkney, but also in the north of Scotland and the Western Isles.

BROCHS Brochs are massive circular dry-stone buildings up to 20m in outside diameter and 13m high. They normally had a solid foundation of bedrock or packed clay, and the first course was also solid with well-built faces and the core filled by packed stone. The exterior wall was *"battered"*, so that the buildings tapered inwards towards the top as the masonry became thinner. The interior wall in contrast did not slope in.

Above the foundation level, the walls were hollow, with stone lintels tying the walls together. Access to higher levels was afforded by stairs and passages. Scarcements built into the inner walls supported floors. There was only one small entrance, normally with a guard cell. Apart from the large amount of stone required, these buildings would also have needed a lot of wood for their interior finishings.

Over a hundred brochs or broch sites have so far been identified in Shetland. The vast majority are coastal, and in prime defensive positions rather than in the heart of agricultural communities. Many had external defences of walls and ditches, but very few had associated contemporary domestic buildings. Many are in spectacular locations which are worth visiting for the walk alone.

PROMONTORY FORTS
Apart from brochs there are two other types of fortified site in Shetland. Promontory forts, where an earth or stone rampart, often with ditches, has been built across a narrow isthmus, are quite common with good examples at Ness of Garth, Sandness, and Brough of Stoal, Yell.

BLOCKHOUSES In some cases forts include a well-built stone blockhouse, as at Scatness. Stone blockhouses may also have some ritual or status function as at Ness of Burgi and Clickimin where they close off an area, but it is hard to see how they were really defensive in a physical sense at least.

Culswick Broch, West Mainland is dramatically situated

Ness of Burgi, Sumburgh - blockhouse and ramparts

DUNS The third type of defensive structure is the dun which is like a small, single-skinned broch and is normally built on a small island with access by causeway. Good examples include those at Burga Water, Sandness and Huxter, Whalsay, which has a blockhouse on its entrance side.

Mousa Broch is uniquely well-preserved

The relationship between duns, blockhouses, ramparts and brochs remains unclear. Until recently there have been no modern investigations of any of these structures. Many brochs have later buildings built into them, or around them, especially those in favourable farming areas, such as Jarlshof, Clickimin, and, of course, Old Scatness. Further examples may well become apparent in future.

Iron Age comb

Recent excavations have shed considerable new light on the broch period and it now seems that some brochs may have been in construction as early as before 200BC and that many were in use for a long time.

Mousa Broch interior

Clickimin broch and blockhouse, Lerwick

IRON AGE TIMELINE

BC	
c.2000	Bronze Age
	Beakers first appear
1500	Peat bogs developing
c.800	Callanish abandoned
700	Iron Age round houses
600	Oldest Broch deposits
100	Brochs at peak
100AD	Brochs abandoned

SITES TO VISIT
BROCHS

Clickimin, Lerwick
Noss Sound, Bressay
Burland, Brindister
Mousa Broch
Burraland, Sandwick
Southpunds, Levenwick
Dalsetter, Boddam
Jarlshof, Sumburgh
Old Scatness, Sumburgh
Culswick, W Mainland
Huxter, Sandness
Houlland, Eshaness

Burra Ness, Yell
Underhoull, Unst
Belmont, Unst

PROMONTORY FORTS

Clickimin, Lerwick
Scatness, Sumburgh
Ness of Burgi, Sumburgh
Ness of Garth, Sandness
Brough of Stoal, Yell

DUNS

Burga Water,Sandness
Loch of Huxter, Whalsay

ARCHAEOLOGY AND HISTORY

Old Scatness broch and surrounding buildings seen from the south

Old Scatness Broch and its associated wheelhouses was first discovered during road-building in 1975. This is the first such site to be investigated in recent years in Shetland, and has yielded much insight into life in Iron Age times as well as into likely dates at which some of the brochs were built. Together with Jarlshof and Mousa it is one of the *"must see"* sites for anyone interested in archaeology

The south end of Mainland Shetland is the most fertile area of the whole island and was clearly well populated in the time of the brochs. Jarlshof is just to the south east, while several other brochs are close-by. There are also promontory forts at Scatness and Ness of Burgi. Old Scatness turns out to be another settlement which was occupied continuously for a very long time - at least 2,500 years.

Ard marks in the soil dating from the Bronze Age are the oldest signs of occupation of the site. The lowest levels of the broch have been dated to somewhere between 400 and 200 BC, while the surrounding aisled wheelhouses date from around 100BC. The Pictish *"figure of 8"* house and the unusual bear symbol carving may date from the 7th or 8th centuries AD, while there was also evidence of Norse and later occupation.

Replicas of various houses have been built next to the site and exhibitions about stone working, spinning, weaving, beer-making and other Iron Age or Viking Age activities help the visitor to appreciate and understand life in these times.

Decorated pebble

5cm

Cross-section of the ditch surrounding the broch

There has been much debate about the origins, dating and purpose of the brochs which until recently has involved immigration of an "elite" who were supposed to have "taken over" and then for some reason of external threat built the brochs, perhaps to defend against Roman slave traders.

View from south east of site, Fitful Head in background

Roman artefacts were in fact found in several brochs, and there are records of visits by Pytheas in about 325BC and Agricola's fleet in AD83 to Orkney. Thus there may well have been contact between Shetland and the Roman Empire during the late Iron Age, but the brochs seem to have been developed well before this time.

It now appears that they may be a building style indigenous to Northern Scotland which occurred shortly after the introduction of iron, which itself would have caused a considerable economic revolution. While it may not be necessary to invoke incomers taking control of society, such imposing buildings as brochs and blockhouses, as well as the numerous promontory forts would not be constructed without good reason.

The period of primary occupation of many of the brochs seems to have been relatively short, but their subsequent usage as handy quarries for wheelhouses, dykes and later buildings lasted until recent times. The high quality of construction, requirement for labour, wood and quarried stone and above all the large number in Shetland, suggest a society with plenty of resources and access to substantial boats, as well as skill in building work not previously seen in the islands.

The Old Scatness broch only came to public knowledge when a JCB driver complained about problems digging out a new access road for the airport control tower - a good comment on the quality of the broch masons' workmanship!

It is unclear whether the Romans ever reached Shetland. In AD83, after the success at the battle of Mons Graupius, Agricola ordered his fleet to circumnavigate Britain, and to *"subdue Orkney"*. His son-in-law, Tacitus quotes *"Dispecta est et Thule..."* - now translated as, *"A close examination of Shetland was also made..."*.

Agricola went to university in Massalia (Marseilles) which was the home town of Pytheas who had explored British waters about 325BC, and is said to have included Shetland in his itinerary. Agricola may well have drawn on Pytheas' confidential reports in planning his circumnavigation and visits to *"subdue"* the Northern Isles. Whether the natives were impressed remains even more in doubt.

Pictish bear symbol

Iron smelting with Iron Age technology

National Museum of Scotland

St Ninian's Isle treasure

The late Iron Age Pictish culture with its distinctive carved symbol stones, cross slabs, expert silverwork and ogam inscriptions flourished in north eastern Scotland and reached Shetland by the 6th century. However, after the grandeur of the brochs, the houses so far found from this time are strangely insignificant.

So far all such buildings excavated in Shetland have been in the vicinity of brochs, including the distinctively Pictish structure at Old Scatness, which may have been a smiddy. A replica can be seen on the site. All of these houses are quite small and so far no large structure from this time has been found.

Several painted quartz stones have been found in Pictish contexts in Shetland as well as Orkney and Caithness. Their use is not known, but the only Pictish burial cairn so far found in Shetland, in Unst, was surrounded by stones and lined inside with quartz pebbles. Perhaps quartz had some religious connotation at this time.

Pictish burial, Unst

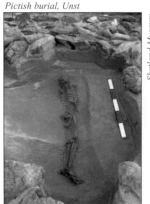

Shetland Museum

Animal-headed figure from Mail

Carved stone with cross

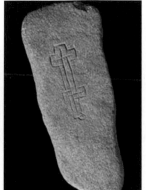

Shetland Museum

Several stones carved with Pictish symbols have been found in Shetland, as well as two cross-slabs, one at Papil on Burra Isle and the other at Cullingsburgh on Bressay. Parts of stone altars or shrines, including corner posts and a front slab carved with figures of monks which may date from the 8th century have also been found.

Ogam-inscribed stone from Mail

The most striking example of Pictish art is the hoard of 28 silver items (plus a Porpoise jawbone), found in 1958 in a larch box under a cross-inscribed stone in the floor of the chapel on St Ninian's Isle. The 11th or 12th century chapel which can be seen today is built on top of a much older Pictish one. It is not known if the dedication is original, proving a link to Whithorn and the Roman Church perhaps in the 6th century, or replaced an earlier one.

The Vikings referred to the Pictish priests or monks as *"Papar"* and there are at least 12 *"Papa"* names in various parts of Shetland. They also used the word *"Petta"* as in Pettadale, which is thought to refer to Picts. The sagas say that Shetland was unoccupied when the Norse arrived, but this seems unlikely. It seems, however, from the scanty domestic evidence so far found that the population may have been quite small.

One theory is that the better-off Picts lived in wooden houses. They are known to have had excellent ships and a powerful navy, based in Burghead, so that it is quite possible that they, like the Vikings later, shipped in timber for construction purposes. The generally acidic soil conditions would ensure that no vestige of this survives today.

Shetland Museum

The Bressay Stone, Obverse

Bressay cross-slab

PICTISH TIMELINE

AD
83 Roman fleet *"subdues"* Orkney
 and perhaps inspects Shetland
c.100 decline of brochs
c.680 first symbol stones
741 Dalriada defeats Picts
742 Norse attack Burghead fort
c.780 St Ninian's Isle hoard
c.800 Norse settlement under way
843 Unification of Picts & Scots
c.880 Norse Earldom established

PICTISH SITES

Old Scatness, Sumburgh
Jarlshof, Sumburgh
Clickimin, Lerwick
Lerwick Museum
St Ninian's Isle
Papil, Burra Isle
Mail cemetery
Cullingsburgh, Bressay
Sandwick, Unst
Underhoull, Unst
National Museum, Edinburgh

The "Monks' Stone", found at Papil

ARCHAEOLOGY AND HISTORY

Jarlshof at Sumburgh is a multi-period site

There is no dated evidence for the first arrival and initial settlement of the **Vikings** in Shetland, but it is logical to assume that this happened after major raiding started in Britain, around 800AD, and probably well into the 9th century.

The limited amount of good agricultural land probably meant that quite small numbers actually settled initially. What is clear is that the existing language was rapidly replaced by Old Norse and virtually all of the place names which exist today are Norse, except for a very few possible older names and some newer ones.

Norse house at East Sandwick, Unst

There are not many archaeological remains from the early settlement time, apart from some modifed Pictish or Iron Age houses, and a few Norse-type artefacts, mostly from burials. Only a small number of non-Christian Norse burials have so far come to light. This may be because of poor preservation of bones and artefacts in the acid soil. Also, all of the Viking burials so far examined have been discovered by chance as there was nothing on the surface to indicate their presence, so that many more may await future archaeologists.

However, at Jarlshof the Norse

period covers the 9th to the 13th centuries, and there is a fascinating jumble of ruined Norse buildings to speculate over. Here the buildings had stone foundations with substantial walls of stone and turf, and thatched roofs. The insides of the houses would have been lined with wood, with paved floors and lined drains.

The living areas had benches along the walls and a central hearth with a separate raised kitchen area. The houses were often enlarged by building more rooms alongside the main structure. The byre was on the downhill end of the building, or else separate. Farms also had small outbuildings, perhaps for storage, hens or pigs, and a small mill on a nearby stream.

Other Norse houses have been excavated on Unst and Papa Stour. The Unst construction resembles that at Jarlshof, but on Papa Stour a Norwegian-style *stofa* was constructed from wood. This leads to speculation that perhaps many of the Norse houses were at least partly wooden, and that timber was shipped from Norway, or

Shetland Museum

38

Scotland. Return cargoes may have been of wool or dried fish. Certainly the Viking *knarrs* were well up to such a job.

The Viking houses are of a much higher standard and scale than the houses so far discovered from Pictish times. It has been suggested that because the Vikings would have picked all the prime sites, themselves most likely occupied by the original inhabitants, most of the ruins would have been rebuilt upon several times over the centuries.

Cows, sheep and ponies were kept, and barley was grown. Fishing was a major activity, and iron fish hooks together with steatite weights were used. Spinning and weaving were also important, as shown by the many spindle whorls and loom weights at Jarlshof. Iron was smelted from bog-iron, and the local blacksmith no doubt made the majority of the items needed

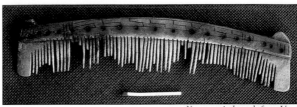
Norse period comb from Unst

by the community.

A large array of high quality Viking artefacts have been found in Shetland, including domestic items like bone combs

Decorated comb case

Shetland Museum

Steatite fishing weight

Norse lamp

Norse house at Jarlshof

VIKING AGE TIMELINE

c.600 Development of longships
late 700s Norse first prominent
790s Viking attacks on Britain
841 Dublin founded
849 Large fleets of Viking
    ships attacking Britain
872 Harald Harfargi sole King
    of Norway, makes Rognvald
    Earl of Orkney & Shetland
875 Rognvald's brother, Sigurd
    the Mighty becomes Earl
893 Torf-Einar, youngest son of
    Rognvald made Earl
963 Earl Thorfinn Skull-splitter
980 Sigurd the Stout Earl
986-989 Sigurd gains control in
    the west, marries daughter of
    Malcolm II of Scotland
995 King Olav Tryggvesson
    forcibly converts Sigurd
c.1000 Discovery of Vinland
1014 Battle of Clontarf
    Thorfinn the Mighty now Earl
1035 Rognvald Brusison joint Earl
1042 Norse in control of west again
1046 Death of Earl Rognvald
1064 Death of Thorfinn
    Joint Earls Paul I & Erlend II
1066 King Harald Hardrada
    killed at Stamford Bridge
1098 King Magnus Barelegs
    expedition to west, Earls Paul
    & Erlend die in Norway

ARCHAEOLOGY AND HISTORY

Norse house interior at Underhoull, Unst

and pins, steatite and pottery utensils, fishing equipment and iron tools. Interestingly, very few weapons have turned up, but this probably reflects the care with which these valuable possessions were treated, rather than their absence.

The Vikings utilised the extensive resources of steatite available at Cunningsburgh and elsewhere in Shetland to make all manner of domestic utensils, seeming to prefer this to pottery.

Several Norse farmsteads have been found on Unst, which is

Norse house passage at Underhoull

fertile, has good harbours and a source of steatite, but is also nearest to Norway and thus likely to be an early landfall. An excavated Norse house lies below the broch at Underhoull, itself built on the ruins of an Iron Age house. No doubt both used the broch as a quarry. Other houses have also been excavated at Hamar and on the shore at East Sandwick.

A document from 1299 which details a dispute between a Papa Stour woman and the local representative of Duke Haakon, and specifies a meeting in the

duke's *stofa* on the island, led to a ground survey and then an excavation of what may be the actual building mentioned. The building excavated had a stone foundation and exterior walls, but the interior was probably wooden, with a planked wooden floor, which dates from about 1100AD.

Up until Viking times grain was milled using hand querns, however *"Norse"* mills were introduced soon after the settlement. These small vertical axis watermills can be seen all over Shetland, and many were in use until quite recently. They generally use small streams as a power source, normally diverted through a lade to power the wheel and drive the millstone. They were referred to as "click" mills due to the noise they made while in operation.

Shetland was administered as part of the Orkney Earldom until after the rising by the Earl of Orkney and others against the Norwegian Crown in 1194, and the ensuing battle of Florvag. It was administered directly from Norway from 1195 onwards. However, there was increasing Scottish influence, especially through the Church, and gradually Norse control was waning. Shetland was to remain firmly under the control of the Norwegian Crown in spite of this for nearly 300 years.

After the Treaty of Perth of 1266, Norway ceded the Hebrides and the *"Kingdom of the Isles"* to Scotland, but its hold on Shetland was to last another 200 years, during which time Scottish interest in the isles steadily increased as a result of the Earldom, Church and trade.

Throughout the Norse period law and order seems to have been important and several *Tings* were established in Shetland. The principal *Law Ting* was held on a small holm at the north end of Tingwall Loch, in the shadow of St Magnus Church. The Norse laws were steadily developed and codified over the years and although the islands were annexed to Scotland in 1471, as late as 1567 they were ratified by the Scottish Parliament.

The Norse legal system was *Udal Law*, where landowners held land themselves, and not ultimately under the king as in feudal law. Some aspects of this law still apply today, particularly with respect to ownership of the foreshore, salmon fishing rights and certain landholdings. Despite attacks from Edinburgh lawyers and politicians over the years, *Udal Law* still survives.

Coped headstone, Framgord, Unst

Bronze jewellery piece

Shetland Museum

Norse-type mill interior, Mousa

Norse-type mill at Huxter, Sandness

Shetland Museum

Norse pot

NORSE TIMELINE

1102 Bishop William installed
c.1104 Earls Haakon & Magnus
1115 Martyrdom of Magnus
1135 Earl Rognvald takes over
c.1151/3 Rognvald at Crusades
1194 Florvag settlement
1195 Direct rule from Norway
1206 Death of Earl Harald, strong ties Norway & Scotland
c.1231 Murder of Earl John - last Norse Earl
c.1233 First Scottish Earl Magnus II
1248 King of Man drowned at Sumburgh Röst with bride - daughter of King Haakon
1263 Battle of Largs
1266 Settlement of Perth
1290 Death of Margaret of Norway
1292 King Erik remarries to sister of Robert the Bruce
c.1336 1st Sinclair Earl - Malise
1349 Plague epidemic
1379 Earl Henry Sinclair I - the last Viking Earl
1400 Earl Henry II - first Scottish nobleman Earl
1420 Thomas Tulloch Bishop & Scottish commissioner
1433 Earliest Scottish charter
1434 Earl William Sinclair
1469 Impignoration
1470 James III buys Earldom - end of Norse Earldom
1471 Annexation by Scotland

NORSE SITES TO VISIT

Law Ting Holm, Tingwall
Jarlshof, Sumburgh
Catpund, Cunningsburgh
Da Biggins, Papa Stour

Gossabrough, Yell
Breakon, Yell
Sandwick, Unst
Belmont, Unst
Underhoull, Unst

ARCHAEOLOGY AND HISTORY

The "Monks' Stone", discovered in 1943 at Papil on West Burra

The **"Monks' Stone"** and corner pieces may date from the 8th century, and certainly when the Vikings arrived they found *"Papar"* at various places in the islands, as shown by placenames. There are many ancient chapel sites in Shetland, but most are ruined, or have been built over several times.

All of these early chapels were small, perhaps only having room for their stone box shrine, and were surrounded by a kirkyard wall, within which there would have been a large crossslab. Most of the devotions probably took place outside which would have been quite in order for people who lived largely outside anyway.

Churches at **Papil** (St Laurence, demolished 1804) and **Tingwall** (St Magnus, demolished c. 1790) had slim towers about 20m high and were similar to the 12th century kirk on Egilsay in Orkney. Sadly these and most other Norse and medieval churches were knocked down in the late 18th century partly because they represented the "old religion" and were a threat to the power of the incoming Scottish ministers, but also because they were ruinous from neglect.

In 995 Earl Sigurd was given the choice of conversion to Christianity or the death of his son by King Olaf Tryggvason - and of course the whole Earldom immediately became "officially" Christian. The Vikings may have tolerated at least some of the *"Papar"*, whose education may have made them useful, and whose place in local society may have made the initial takeover easier.

Soon many new and refurbished churches were built and the first Bishop of Orkney installed. Although only first mentioned in 1215, Shetland would have had an Archdeacon, or representative of the bishop, soon after to take charge of the clergy locally. He probably had the St Magnus Church at Tingwall as his base, next to the Law Ting.

Of the remaining churches, the chancel arch of **St Mary's** in Sand (HU347472) and the much more intact **St Olaf's** at Lundawick (HP567041) in Unst are perhaps the most impressive. **St Mary's** (HU521422) at Cullingsburgh (HU521423) on Bressay is also interesting but the transepts are 17th century.

At most of the other sites all that remains is a mound, perhaps with wall footings, in graveyards or next to newer churches. Many of these buildings were substantially intact when visited in the late 18th or 19th century. In some cases the churches were

Shrine corner post from St Ninian's

The 12th century chapel on St Ninian's Isle

expanded and refurbished, so that elements of older structures may remain.

In Norse times the Bishop was under the Cathedral of Nidaros, but as Scottish influence increased by the late 13th century the Bishop was Scottish, and in 1472 the Bishopric was transferred to St Andrews. The Reformation in 1560 was to finally abolish all church links with Norway.

St Olaf's Kirk, Lundawick, Unst dates from the 12th century

Remains of Cross Kirk, Eshaness, demolished by a minister who feared it

Cross-slab from Bressay

St Mary's Chapel chancel arch

OLD CHURCHES TIMELINE

AD
563 Columba on Iona
995 Sigurd's conversion
1472 Bishopric to St Andrews
1560 Reformation
1790 St Magnus kirk demolished

SITES TO VISIT

St Mary's, Bressay
Papil, West Burra
St Magnus, Tingwall
St Ninian's Isle
Lunna Church, N Mainland
St Olaf's, Voe
Kame of Isbister, Northmavine
Kirk Holm, Sand
St Ninian's Isle, S Mainland
St Mary's, Sand
Cross Kirk, Eshaness

Birrier of West Sandwick, Yell
Kirk of Ness, Breakon, Yell
Framgord, Unst
St Olaf's, Lunda Wick, Unst
St John's Balliasta, Unst
Blue Mull, Unst
Strandburgh, Fetlar

18th century chuch at Lunna

UDAL LAW

In 1910 Orkney & Shetland Swans were shown not to belong to the Crown

Udal Law, from ON *odal* - land held in allodial tenure, is the ancient Norse system of inheritance and law which the Vikings brought wherever they settled. No trace remains of the previous legal system, which no doubt derived from the distant past with influences from previous incomers, but it seems that the Norse took over control of an existing pattern of settlement.

About 1037 King Magnus the Good and in 1274 King Magnus Lagabote *(the Lawmender)* supervised revision and codification of the old laws, which of course applied to Orkney and Shetland as part of Norway.

Udal Law is totally different to Scots Law. *Udallers* have absolute ownership of their land, with no superior, gained by holding the land over a number of generations, normally originally by settlement. This land was held in freehold, often unwritten, with no obligation except a duty to pay tax or *skat* to the king. The eldest son inherited the father's house, while the rest of the property was shared among siblings, daughters inheriting half as much as sons. Over the years this led to an extreme fragmentation of land ownership and, despite

reform, left *Udallers* wide open to exploitation.

The fact that no written documents were required to substantiate possession greatly confused the Scots. The lack of Title Deeds was much used by Scottish "landlords" and their lawyers, as one of the means of grabbing lands from the real owners. Considerable amounts of hill land are still held in this ancient manner, which can cause problems for public bodies at times.

There was a policy on the part of the Scottish Crown to acquire the *Udal* rights to land, because although the Scottish Parliament had "abolished" Norse Law in 1611, this could not be retrospective. Indeed, in view of the pawned nature of the islands any Scottish Act over the Norse Law even now may be in doubt. Steadily Scots "landowners" acquired "ownership" of *Udal* lands by often dubious means, until the Udallers were very much reduced. Ironically this was eventually to lead to the downfall of the incoming laird class themselves.

The fundamental difficulty with Scotland was that the King was nominally the owner of all of the land, which was held by landlords

with the Crown as superior, and with services and payments to be made, as well as a written title, whereas the *Udal* system was virtually the direct opposite. This remains incomprehensible to Edinburgh lawyers, well versed in Feudal Law but not in *Udal Law*. However, now that the Scottish Parliament has abolished Feudal Law, interest has revived in the older laws.

Udal Law still exists today, most apparent in the ownership of the coastline. Whereas in the rest of Britain ownership of land extends only to the High Water mark, in Orkney and Shetland this extends to the lowest spring ebb, plus variously as far as a stone can be thrown, or a horse can be waded, or a salmon net can be thrown. This has enormous implications to building work, inshore fisheries and piers. Also anything arriving fortuitously on the shore is technically the property of the landowner.

Since the foreshore belongs to the adjacent landowner and is not Common Land, there is no absolute right of access to the intertidal zone in Orkney or Shetland. However, traditionally no one objects - if in doubt it is polite to ask. Norse ownership of the sea and seabed is claimed by some to have extended out to the *Marebekke*. he edge of the Continental Shelf - ownership of fishing, sealing and whaling rights were and remain important.

Although in 1468 Orkney and in 1469 Shetland were impignorated (mortgaged) to Scotland, and annexed in 1472, there have been many confirmations of the recognition of *"Norse Laws"* including by the Scottish Parliament in 1567. Further, in 1667, the Treaty and Peace of Breda confirmed the right of redemption was unprescribed and thus unprescribable.

Various cases during the 20th century confirmed the primacy of *Udal Law* in certain instances, while others did not. Whereas ownership of the foreshore seems to be accepted, the position regarding the sea and seabed is undecided. In all cases to date the Scottish High Court has ruled that the Crown owns these assets, but it is hard to see how the Crown can rule in such a case.

accompanied by his friend, the Procurator Fiscal, went out to Harray Loch and shot a Swan. The case went to the High Court and the Crown lost. Everywhere else in UK the Crown owned the Swans - in Orkney and Shetland they were, and still are, the property of the people. Nowadays we do not shoot Swans, but the principles of the old Norse *Udal Law* still stand.

Udal Law was invoked in a 1965 attempt to keep the St Ninian's Isle Treasure in Shetland when the Crown claimed it as treasure trove. Not unnaturally the Crown's courts found in favour of itself, and now the Pictish silver languishes in Edinburgh, while visitors to

dispense when the landowner realised that his rights had been infringed. Thus state ignorance of *Udal Law* continues to this day.

The Crown had to admit the supremacy of *Udal Law* in this respect and refund their charges in favour of the actual landowner. Thus there has been little change in the attitude of Edinburgh lawyers in the last 600 years - they still treat the *Udal Law* with contempt - hopefully at their continued peril!

In 1990 the Court of Session ruled against Shetland Salmon Farmers Association and Lerwick Harbour Trust in their claim that the Crown could not own the seabed around the Northern Isles. The blatant farce of the Crown ruling for itself was of course ignored by politicians at the time.

The current debate about *Udal Law* has been fired by the attempt of the Crown estate to charge very large sums of "rent" for a new fibre optic cable to link Orkney and Shetland with Iceland and Scotland. Along with local concerns about the control of fishing and fish farming, it seems that the Crown is going to have a hard time until a constitutional settlement of Orkney and Shetland's status is finally achieved - after well over 500 years of impignoration.

Shetlanders still like to think that the classless society of today derives from the *Udal* tradition, where every man is equal, but also every man has an equal duty to society. Today's Shetlander may be a mixture of Norse, Scots and others, but he or she is nevertheless still independent by nature.

Udal Law was upheld in the "Queen's Hotel" case of 1903

When the owner of the Queens Hotel argued that he owned the foreshore, this was upheld in 1903, when Lerwick Harbour Trustees claimed that they held the land under a Crown grant. However, a similar case in 1953 was won by the Trustees on the basis that the property was *feudal*, a status which applies to some Shetland property.

One anomaly is the Mute Swan. In Orkney about 1910 a Kirkwall lawyer was determined to prove that Udal Law still had force, and

Shetland can only see pale imitations.

In the mid-1970s when the Occidental Oil Company was building its pipeline to Flotta, it negotiated with the Crown Estate for rights to cross the foreshore at the end of the 4th Barrier at Cara without realising that the Crown has no authority over the intertidal zone in Orkney. The Company had apparently even paid the Crown Commissioners for a privilege that they had no authority to

SHETLAND LANGUAGE

Puffins are known locally as "Tammy Nories" which is also the nickname for the Foula folk

Shetlanders speak with a distinctive accent and use many dialect expressions which derive from a mixture of the Old Norse language of the Vikings and Lowland Scottish English. Although gradually over the centuries English replaced Norn its influence is still pervasive in both the spoken language and placenames of Shetland.

Throughout the book suggested derivations of placenames are included, some of which are certain and others more speculative. Even the experts do not agree on many, but it is clear that very few predate the arrival of the Vikings. Many others are translations of varying correctness into English from Norn.

Other influences on *"Shetlandic"* have included Dutch fishermen, German merchants and seamen, and continued connections with Norway and Faeroe, but by far the biggest input has been English in the form of Lowland Scots.

Thus, while the Shetlander will use a very clear form of English to communicate with visitors, those new to the dialect may well find speech between native Shetlanders outside Lerwick quite hard to follow at first.

Meeting Sheep

Hit's guid tae meet sheep, whin gaan ipo a vaige du'll meet blyde folk at da end o'him

"It is good to meet sheep when on a journey - you'll meet fine folk at the end of it."

A Toast to the Fiddler

Hurra fur da Fiddler Lang may he live Tae dra da bow Never may he die!

A Fisherman's Toast

Here's death ta da heid at wears nae hair!

(A variation on *"Death to the French!"*)

A Traditional Shetland Toast

Here's ta dee and dy folk, fae me an my folk An I hope it whin dee and dy folk meets me an my folk at dee and dy folk is a blyde ta see me an my folk as me an my folk is at seean dee an dy folk

SHETLAND FISH RECIPES

Fish has always featured strongly in the Shetland diet. Before the advent of steam transport fish could only be brought to market in a preserved state - either salted, or salted and dried. The fishermen retained the heads, livers, roe, stomachs and air bladders for their own consumption. Today these parts are normally discarded at sea, but as the writer can attest they can make delicious meals.

KRAPPIT HEID

Large Cod's head, 500g Haddock livers, 200g oatmeal, 100g flour, salt, pepper. (Cod or Ling livers may also be used.) Rinse out head under cold water. Remove any worms from livers and knead into a pulp with the oatmeal, add flour and mix well. Hold mouth open with a spoon and ladle in mixture. Place in pan of cold water and boil gently for 30-60 minutes, depending on the size of the head(s). The dish is served with boiled potatoes, and is said to be so filling that partakers will not have to eat for at least 12 hours.

STAP

250g Haddock and 125g livers per person. Poach fish and livers gently, skin and bone the fish, mash with the livers, season and eat. Simple but delicious.

SILLOCKS AND PILTOCKS

Saithe or Coalfish are common around Shetland's coastline. The young are called Sillocks and normally fried in butter, perhaps with oatmeal, just after being caught as they do not keep well. Piltacks are year-old fish, and are excellent when fresh. They can be boiled immediately they are taken ashore and then eaten cold in the morning for breakfast.

LIVER CUIDS

Piltocks cleaned through the gills rather than being split open, are stuffed with Cod liver, and a small new potato is used to seal the gullet. The fish are then grilled or baked with a little butter.

OILY MUGGIES

Cod's stomach stuffed with Cod's liver mixed with oat meal and flour is a variation on Krappit Head. It is said that when you spat in the fire after eating this delicacy the flames would flare up on account of the oiliness of the livers.

SHETLAND PARISH NICK-NAMES
(*Tee* Names)

Lerwick	*Whitings*
Scalloway	*Sma Drink*
Bressay	*Sparks, Sharks* or *Crackers* (good talkers)
Burra	*Liver Muggies*
Cunningsburgh	North - *Yaks*; South - *Turks*
Dunrossness	*Bannocks,* or *Liver Coids* (Piltocks stuffed with cod liver)
Tingwall	*Bleddick Spoots,* or *Timmer Guns*
Weisdale	*Gaats* (cut pigs)
Aithsting	*Smuiks* or *Smocks* (sewn cloth shoes)
Sandsting	*Suck o'Legs*
Mid Waas	*Gentry* or *Jantry*
Wast O'Waas	*Settlins*
Doon O'Waas	*Dirt*
Sandness	*Burstin Brunis* (oatmeal or beremeal cakes)
Nesting	*Gauts* (cut pigs)
Lunnasting	*Hoes* (dogfish)
Delting	*Sparls* (smoked and dried sheep sausage)
Northmavine	*Liver (Oily) Muggies* (cod stomach stuffed with its liver)
Yell	*(Sheep) Thieves*
Unst	*Midden Slues* (lazy, unclean people)
Fetlar	*Russie Foals* (shaggy young horses)
Whalsay	*Piltocks* (young coal fish or cuithes)
Skerries	*Lings*
Papa Stour	*Scories* (Young Gulls)
Foula	*(Tammy) Nories* (Puffins)

The Lord's Prayer in 18th century Norn

Fyvor o er i Chimeri,
Halaght vara nam dit.
La Koningdum din kumma,
La vill din vera guerde,
i Vrildin sinda er i Chimeri.
Gav vus dagh u dagloght brau.
Forgive sindor wara sin vi forgiva
dem ao sinda 'gainst wus.
Lia wus eke o vera tempa,
but delivra wus fra adlu idlu.
For do i ir Koningdum,
u Puri, u Glori, Amen.

Scalloway Castle was built by forced labour about 1599

Shetland became part of Scotland in 1469, by Impignoration *(placed in pawn, held in pledge until redeemed by payment of the outstanding amount)*. In fact, a process of *"Scottification"* had been in progress for a long time. All of the Earldom lands in Shetland had been taken by the Norwegian Crown in 1195, but the Orkney Earls certainly came to own land in Shetland during the succeeding centuries, and especially during the time of the Sinclair and Stewart Earls.

The Earls had always had a problem with *"dual allegiance"* to Norway and Scotland, and never more so than during the crisis of 1263 leading up to the Battle of Largs and the **Treaty of Perth of 1266**

when the Hebrides and Isle of Man were ceded to Scotland, which was then meant to make an annual payment to Norway of 100 marks.

By 1460 this *"annual"* had been unpaid for years and was a serious issue. It was resolved that the daughter of King Christian (of Denmark who now also ruled Norway and Sweden) should marry the son of James II, later James III. The Scots demanded Orkney and Shetland as part of the dowry and eventually the impecunious King Christian agreed to pledge first Orkney in 1468 for 50,000 florins and then Shetland in 1469 for another 10,000 florins.

In fact the land handed over was limited to royal land, as the king

had no rights over church land or *udal* land, which would include land owned by the Earl. He did however transfer sovereignty and the rights to receive taxes to the Scottish Crown. In 1470 James II purchased all rights and lands of the Earldom from William Sinclair for the Scottish Crown.

In 1472 the Scottish Parliament annexed Orkney and Shetland. Further legislation followed, but never quite destroyed all of the old Norse *Udal Laws*. However, despite many attempts, neither did the Danes succeed in regaining the Northern Isles. There was to follow a period of property acquisition by Scots, by fair means or foul, combined with tension between the Sinclair and later Stewart Earls and the smaller landowners.

Robert Stewart was the illegitimate son of James V and was first granted Orkney and Shetland in 1565. This unpleasant, but cultured villain and his son, Patrick were to cause much hardship and oppression in Shetland for the next 50 years. Scalloway Castle was built by forced labour in about 1599, but open abuse of their powers by the Stewarts and their underlings by expropriating land and property and extorting taxes was perhaps worse.

Patrick's execution in 1615 was for rebellion and treason, not oppression, but after this Shetland became a remote backwater as far as Scotland was concerned, except when the

Royal Navy needed crews in the Napoleonic and 20th century wars and of course when North Sea Oil arrived and then the interest was tax.

From the 17th century onwards Scottish Law, Landowners and Church prevailed. Although there were some notable exceptions, especially in the Church, there was serious oppression from Scottish "landlords", most of whose rights to "their" land were highly dubious.

The *"truck"* system whereby crofters usually paid their rent in kind, whether dried fish, knitwear, butter, meat or other produce, and had to buy their few domestic necessities as well as fishing gear and tools from the laird's shop was quite iniquitous. The *Haaf* fishery which developed from about 1700 was to increase this dependence, but the Dutch and Napoleonic Wars followed by Whaling and Herring Fishing were to bring Shetland much more into the centre of things, and allowed many small traders to set up in business, thus breaking the monopoly of the *truck* system.

The population reached an unsustainable maximum of

Clipper schooners such as "Matchless" took several days to reach Shetland

31,670 in 1861, but from the 1830s until the passing of the Crofters' Act in 1886 there were clearances to create large farms. Even if not cleared from their land, hardship caused large numbers of people to emigrate, especially to New Zealand and Canada. Population decline was going to continue until the 1970s when it reached a low of 17,000, but the arrival of North Sea Oil and the development of the fishing industry was to transform Shetland yet again.

Regular all-year round transport to Scotland arrived with the steamship in 1858. Suddenly this was to open up whole new markets for Shetland ponies, cattle, sheep, fish and knitwear. Prior to this the journey on small sailing smacks could easily take a week.

The first school was set up in 1713, and by 1820 more than 90 per cent of the population were literate, even though it was 1827 before each parish was to have a school. Shetlanders have always been keen on learning, and remain so.

SCOTTISH TIMELINE

1560	Scottish Reformation - Church of Scotland moves in
1565	Robert Stewart granted lands in Orkney & Shetland
1577	Complaint by Shetlanders about Bruce
1599	Scalloway Castle built
1593	Death of Robert Stewart
1615	Execution of Patrick Stewart
1620	Privy Council enquiry
1630	Norse still prevalent
1653	English attack Dutch Herring busses at Lerwick
1655	Lerwick Fort started
1673	Dutch burn fort
1700s	Norn much reduced
1703	French burn 100 Dutch Herring busses at Lerwick
1707	Union of Parliaments, decline of German trade
mid 1700s	Arctic whaling boom, *Haaf* fishing increasing
late 1700s	Smallpox controlled, rapid population growth starts Kelp burning begins
1820s	First clearances
1840s and 1850s	Famine and building of *"meal"* roads
1858	First all year steamer
1872	*"Truck"* enquiry *"Shetland Times"* established
1877	*"Earl of Zetland I"* in service
1886	Crofters' Act

St Rognvald II (1901) in Busta Voe, Delting; sixareen flitboat off the bows

Shetland Museum

HISTORY AND CULTURE

Hanseatic Booth, The Pier House, Symbister, Whalsay

The seas around Shetland have been known for their abundance of fish ever since the first people arrived over 5,000 years ago. It was the arrival of the Vikings that saw the first industrial-scale fishing. As early as the 10th century Fife fishermen were catching Herring in the North Sea. By the 12th century the Dutch had started to venture north, and were paying harbour dues to the Orkney Earldom.

During Norse times most trading was done through Bergen, when a considerable amount of salted, dried fish was exported to Norway. During the 15th century, German *Hansa* merchants start-ed to come to Shetland every year, arriving in May, when they set up trading *"booths"* from which they traded fishing gear, meal, salt, alcohol, tobacco and sundry goods for fish, butter and other products.

The *Hansa* traders arrived in increasing numbers from towns such as Bremen, Hamburg, Danzig and Lubeck in Germany during the following centuries. The main export at this time was dried and salted Cod, Ling and Tusk, which found a ready market in Europe. The trade brought much needed cash to the crofter-fishermen and competition ensured a fair deal to all.

After the Union of Parliaments in 1707 the introduction of new taxes made the trade unprof-itable for the merchants and so ended a mutually beneficial relationship after 300 years. A locally promoted white fishery soon developed to replace the German merchants. This is an example of how decisions made far away can have highly detri-mental effects on places like Shetland, a practice which con-tinues today, but also of how local enterprise can circumvent such issues.

By 1400 the Dutch were using larger vessels, called *"busses"*, and salting their catches on board, which meant they could go further afield and for longer. Fishing started on St John's Day, 24th June, and large numbers of Herring busses would accumu-late in Lerwick Harbour whilst awaiting the start of the season. The Dutch traded with the Shetlanders, who exchanged their much valued warm socks, gloves, hats and jumpers for var-ious essential goods, including alcohol, and later, tobacco.

When the Dutch first started to use Lerwick as a forward base there was no settlement in the area, which was nothing but a stoney hill facing the best har-bour in the north. Soon a row of huts developed which were used for trading, storing goods, and "other activities". There was no fishing on Sundays when the whole fleet would return to port.

Fort Charlotte was first built in 1665, during the rule of Oliver Cromwell, to defend Lerwick

Fort Charlotte was first built in 1655, and burnt by the Dutch in 1673

during the Dutch Wars. It was sacked by the Dutch in 1673, after which it was ruinous for over 100 years. This now seems ironic since French warships subsequently attacked the Dutch fishing fleet at Lerwick causing much damage.

The Dutch fishery reached its peak in the 17th and 18th centuries when hundreds of busses would be present at times. The various wars caused setbacks, but the Dutch fishery never really recovered from the effects of the Napoleonic Wars, after which it was Scottish and English fishermen who dominated the herring fishing, although the Dutch still came in force until WWI.

In the late 19th century Herring fishing suddenly grew in importance, and many stations for processing the catches were set up. The main centres were Baltsound in Unst, Lerwick and Scalloway and each season thousands of shore workers and fishermen arrived.

During this time the Herring stations were a hive of activity, with hundreds of boats landing their catches, which were processed and packed with salt into barrels by women, and exported to Germany and Russia in large quantities. The boom lasted until the First World War, after which the markets for salt Herring in Eastern Europe never recovered.

Herring fishing did not get started again until the 1960s, when the purse seine net allowed huge amounts of pelagic fish, such as

Lerwick Harbour crowded with Dutch Herring drifters in the 1890s

Shetland Museum

Dutch Herring sailing drifter

Shetland Museum

Herring and Mackerel to be caught very efficiently using large vessels. Today there is a substantial Shetland fleet of these boats, most of which are based in Whalsay. Once again Herring is being exported in quantity from Shetland.

These knitted gloves and hat found in a peat bog are perhaps similar to items traded with the Dutch

National Museum

National Museum

FISHING TIMELINE

c.1300 Start of Hanseatic trade Bergen
c.1400 Dutch Herring busses
1415 First Hanseatic Shetland trade
c.1500 Dutch start Herring fishing
c.1730 Start of *Haaf* fishery
c.1750 London merchants buy fish
c.1820 Decked sloops appear. offshore Cod fishery develops
1870s Start of Herring boom
1881 Gloup disaster
1900 Delting disaster
1914 End of Herring boom
1940s Seine nets introduced
1959 Fish plant at Scalloway
1965 Herring fishing restarts
1960s Purse seine nets
1980s Rapid growth in pelagic catch
1990s Development of whitefish stock conservation methods

FISHING - SITES TO VISIT

Lerwick Harbour and Museum
Baltsound
Haroldswick Boat Haven
Scalloway Museum
Scalloway Fisheries College
Whalsay

"Far Haaf" a replica sixareen at Baltasound, Unst

***HAAF* FISHING** Fishing was done inshore with handlines until after 1700 when longlines were introduced and the boats started to venture further afield, and stay at sea for several days. After the loss of the German market, the landowners suddenly needed to market fish and other produce themselves and so the *"truck"* system developed, whereby crofter-fishermen were tied to their (normally Scottish) landlords, who supplied boats and gear in return for the right to buy the catch at the end of the year. This was to result in hardship for the people who no longer had the option of trading with outside merchants.

The *sixareens* used in this fish-ery were small open boats less than 10m long, powered by oars or sail. Although very graceful, they were really not suited to off-shore work. There were several serious disasters when storms blew up suddenly, which tragically resulted in the loss of boats and crews, most notably in 1832 and 1881.

The **"*Haaf* Fishery"** (ON *haaf*-ocean) lasted for much of the 18th and 19th centuries, until the undecked *sixareens* were replaced by much larger fully decked smacks which were safer and could stay at sea much longer. In the 19th century there was a short-lived Cod fishery boom, when local vessels ranged as far as Iceland and the Faeroes, but this only lasted till about 1900. The development of the steam trawler made longlining from even these larger sailing boats uneconomic.

SEAMEN Ever since the first settlers arrived the men of the Northern Isles were seamen, and as shipping grew in importance, whether merchant or naval, this ensured that they were in demand as crewmen and officers. There is a long tradition of *"going to sea"* in Shetland. The Shetlanders were always keen on having their children educated, which allowed many to escape the poverty of the croft and become Master Mariners.

WHALING The Basques were probably the first to catch whales in the Arctic, in the 16th century, but by the 17th Dutch and British had also started this "fishery". The whales were processed for the large quantities of oil which could be obtained from their blubber. Whaling ships regularly called at Lerwick to take on crew and supplies before departing for Greenland or Jan Mayen Land. Shetlanders were much sought after to handle the small skiffs used in catching whales, which was very hazardous.

In the early 20th century the Norwegians were encouraged by the British Government to start whaling operations from Shetland and also from the Western Isles. Public objections and a lack of whales soon put a stop to this and the First World War effectively put an end to this unpopular and smelly activity. It

Sixareens at anchor, Fethaland, Northmavine

Shetland Museum

is interesting that it was Norwegian public opinion that stopped the processing of whales there - due to the very bad smell produced.

The Norwegians then turned their attention to the Southern Ocean, and many Shetlanders were to serve on the whaling ships there between 1904 and 1963 when the slaughter finally ended.

NAVAL WARFARE During the 18th and 19th centuries and especially the Napoleonic Wars, the Royal Navy grew immensely in size, and had a huge requirement for crews. Many Shetlanders were to serve under Nelson along with Orcadians and men from the Western Isles. While some were "pressed" into service, many also volunteered. As in the Merchant Navy their abilities as seamen were greatly valued. Up to 5,000 Shetlanders were in the Royal Navy at this time.

MERCHANT NAVY During both World Wars as well as in peacetime Shetlanders played a very large part in the Merchant Navy, with very many ship's Captains, officers and crewmen serving all over the world. As a result Shetland had disproportionately high casualties for its population with about 600 men lost in WWI and 357 in WWII - the vast majority of whom were sunk on merchant ships. In fact one out of six seamen did not return in WWII. Shetland had the highest per capita casualty rate of any county in Britain.

British naval cannon as used in the Napoleonic Wars

Flitting peats by small boat

Shetland Museum

Whaler at anchor, Lerwick Harbour

Shetland Museum

RMS Oceanic

In 1904 part of the German Grand Fleet ominously visited Shetland and lay off the Knab at Lerwick. Royal Navy ships also increasingly made appearances and exercises took place in northern waters. At the start of war the 10th Cruiser Squadron was based in Shetland, and used Swarbacks Minn as an anchorage.

The White Star liner, **RMS Oceanic** (II), was built in 1899, and at 17,272 tons and 214m in length, was the largest ship in the world. With her twin screws and 28,000 SHP she cruised at 19kt, burning nearly 500 tons of coal a day. In August 1914 she was commandeered by the Navy to serve as an armed merchant cruiser in the 10th Cruiser Squadron.

The civilian crew was augmented by naval officers and men, including Captain Slayter, who was in nominal command, with Captain Smith in an advisory capacity. She was sent to Scapa Flow for training and then to patrol between Shetland and the Faeroes. During her first sortie she searched the area around Foula, with a zigzag course to avoid submarines. Thick fog, and confusion about who was in charge led to serious navigational errors and on September 8 she

grounded on the Hoevdi Rocks south east of Foula on a calm and clear day. The tide had swung her stern first onto the well-charted shoal and she stuck fast.

The trawler *Glenogil* and *HMS Forward* attempted to pull her off to no effect, the crew abandoned ship, and on September 11 she was declared lost. On 29 September there was a fierce storm which collapsed the ship. In 1924, most of what was left was salvaged. In the 1970s divers salvaged the remains, including the impressive propellor blade at Lerwick Museum.

The story stands as a sad reminder of the waste and ineptitude of war. Of course the captains were exonerated and the navigation officer received a gentle reprimand. Probably White Star were quite happy to be paid for their fine, but already obsolescent ship.

The object was to stop and search neutral and other ships which might be carrying goods bound for Germany. To do this large, fast ships were needed, and armed passenger liners were deemed to be well suited to the task. In addition to the *Oceanic*, the *Alcantara* was lost off the north of Unst when she attacked the armed merchant ship, *Greif*. Both ships were lost in the action which followed. Yet another such liner, *HMS Avenger,* was also torpedoed off Shetland.

Boom defence nets were installed at the North and South Mouths of Lerwick Harbour and coastal defence guns were placed on Vementry, at the Knab, and in two places on Bressay. The 6-inch guns on Bressay and

Swarbacks Minn is a large, sheltered bay on the west side of Shetland

Vementry remain in their very exposed sites as monuments to war.

Although surface raiders were a problem, the biggest naval threat was submarines. They cheekily used remote voes such as Whalefirth and Ronas Voe as boltholes to hide from Allied ships, to rest and charge batteries. Local shipping was not spared - in 1915 a U-boat surfaced and sank 15 fishing boats near Skerries, but allowed the crews to save themselves, while in 1918 the *St Clair* was attacked but survived on its way to Lerwick. The *St Magnus* was less lucky, and was sunk off Peterhead by a torpedo.

The belated adoption of well-escorted convoys reduced but did not entirely remove the danger from submarines. Later in the war patrols by flying boats and floatplanes were to play an important part in finding U-boats. From 1916 Naval Air Stations were being established and by 1918 the Houton station in Scapa Flow was able to cover as far north as Foula.

A small station was established at Catfirth north east of Lerwick, from where patrols were operated further north. The war was over before this station became fully operational. Although flying boats were very new at the time, they proved most effective at finding U-boats, and sometimes sinking them.

Shetland Museum

German High Seas Fleet at Lerwick, 1904

Six-inch naval gun on Muckle Ward, Vementry, overlooking Swarbacks Minn

Shetland Museum

Naval rating beside Vementry guns

Shorts seaplane taking off

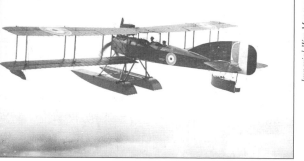

Imperial War Museum

Restored WWII Norwegian fishing boat "Heland" visiting Lerwick, 2003

The *"Shetland Bus"* operated from Shetland during WWII, initially from Lunna on the east side of the Mainland, and then from Scalloway. The story reads like the script of a war movie, except that the exploits actually happened.

Shetland Bus memorial, Scalloway

In April 1940 Norway surrendered to overwhelming German force. Many servicemen escaped to Britain and in the months that followed many more people escaped by small boat, mostly to Shetland. By summer 1941 the *"Shetland Bus"* was in operation, utilising some of the small Norwegian fishing boats which had escaped to operate a clandestine service carrying agents, weapons, radios and explosives to Norway for use in resisting the Germans. People were also ferried back to Britain after operations, for training or to avoid immediate danger of capture.

In 1942 the base moved to Scalloway, but losses were heavy in the first winter, and operations were suspended until more suitable vessels were found. Three US Navy submarine chasers operated from October 1943 and proved very successful in evading German attacks. The vessels were named *Hessa*, *Hitra* and *Vigra* and could do 22 knots. The *Hitra* has been fully restored by the Norwegian Navy and has visited Shetland.

The real achievement of the operation was to persuade the Germans that they needed to maintain a large garrison of over 300,000 men and build a network of coastal defence batteries, the *"Festung Norway"*, as well as station far more aircraft and ships there than really necessary. The result was to tie down a large amount of German military resources which otherwise could been have deployed elsewhere.

The *"Shetland Bus"* was also of much benefit to the Norwegians in occupied Norway who gained a great deal from knowing that the allies were doing something and had not forgotten about them. The steady flow of materials and people combined with the great bravery and often sacrifice of those involved was a huge morale booster. By the end of the war there were at least 60 clandestine radio operators at work sending back intelligence. Apart from the *"Shetland Bus"* many other marine operations were conducted against occupied Norway from Shetland.

Explosives and weapons were hidden in oil drums and packing cases

From late 1942 until 1945 a flotilla of Norwegian motor torpedo boats (MTBs) was based at Lerwick. Heavily armed and capable of 30 knots, they were very successful at harrying coastal shipping and defences. Although the material effect on the war may have been small, the pin-pricks added to the pressure on the Germans.

Lerwick was also used as an advance base for submarines operating in northern waters. They were used to land agents, attack German shipping, watch for capital ships such as *Tirpitz* and to help guard convoys to Russia. One of these, *HMS Venturer*, was the first and only submarine ever to sink another submarine while both were submerged when she torpedoed the *U864* off Bergen in February 1945.

While Shetland's role in the naval aspect of WWII was not as grand as that of Scapa Flow in Orkney, it was nevertheless a very important part of the war in the North Atlantic. It also renewed Shetland's Norwegian links. The *"Shetland Bus"* is now history but the connection with Norway is both historic and very much part of the present.

This was made clear in June 2003, when a large party of Norwegians, some of whom arrived on two fishing boats and the torpedo chaser *Hitra* which took part in many of the wartime exploits, attended the unveiling of a memorial on the Scalloway seafront to those lost in the *"Shetland Bus"* operation .

Shetland Museum

Norwegian fishing boat at Scalloway in WWII

Berger Arnesen, Leif Larsen and Richard Angel, winter 1943-44

Shetland Museum

Restored WWII torpedo chaser "Hitra" at Scalloway

Prince Olav slipway - memorial to Leif Larsen

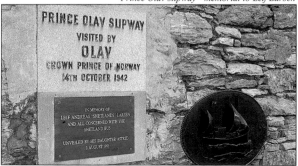

Catalina over Bressay

Sullom Voe was established as an RAF Coastal Command base in 1939, and throughout WWII *Sunderlands* and *Catalinas* patrolled the Atlantic. Their main function was to find and sink submarines, as well as convoy escort. The patrols covered a vast area of ocean from Iceland to the North Cape, and played a major part in the Battle of the Atlantic.

The *SS Manela* was moored at Sullom Voe as an accommodation and supply base until shoreside facilities were built, and *HMS Coventry*, an AA cruiser,

was also based in the Voe until AA gunsites were completed.

The area has the dubious distinction of taking the first bomb to explode on British soil in WWII, on 13 November 1939. Fighter cover was available from Sumburgh and then from nearby Scatsta, but since the Germans tended to come in very low, little warning was given, and there were only a few interceptions.

Nearby **Scatsta** airfield was built by Zetland County Council for the Air Ministry in 1940. Its main function was support of

adjacent Sullom Voe, but it also served as a very useful diversion for aircraft engaged on operations over Norway. Its construction involved removing about 400,000m³ of peat and used over 100,000 tons of stone. A huge variety of aircraft used the airfield during the war.

Sumburgh was first used in 1933 by Captain Fresson of Highland Airways, who started scheduled flights in 1936. In 1939 three *Gladiator* biplanes were based there, as it was then not suitable for other aircraft. By 1941 three runways were ready,

Sunderland at Sullom Voe

Sullom Voe 1939 - SS Manela and a Saro London flying boat

Shetland Museum

and the airfield was to see a lot of wartime activity, mostly anti-submarine and shipping protection patrols. Small numbers of fighters were also based here and succeeded in shooting down several enemy aircraft including the *HE111* of which parts still remain on Fair Isle.

Pin-prick attacks by German aircraft based in Norway continued for some time, but caused little damage. The worst attacks were in December 1941 and January 1942 when air attacks on Fair Isle South Lighthouse resulted in the deaths of two lighthouse keepers' wives, a child and a gunner manning a nearby AA gun, as well as considerable structural damage.

Shetland had several radar stations in WWII, including on Fair Isle, Bressay and Unst, and at Sumburgh among other sites. Large numbers of soldiers were also present on guard duties.

Shetland Museum

Gladiator and pilots, Sumburgh 1940

Shetland Museum

Crater from first bomb of WWII on UK soil - Sullom Voe 13 November 1939

Fair Isle South Light - memorial plaque

Remains of Heinkel HE111 on Fair Isle

FAIR ISLE SOUTH LIGHTHOUSE

BUILT: 1892

ENGINEER: DAVID A. STEVENSON

AUTOMATED: 31ST MARCH 1998

DURING AN AIR ATTACK IN DECEMBER 1941, MRS. CATHERINE SUTHERLAND (AGED 22) THE WIFE OF AN ASSISTANT LIGHTHOUSE KEEPER, WAS KILLED AND THEIR INFANT DAUGHTER SLIGHTLY HURT.

ON 21ST JANUARY 1942 DURING A SECOND ATTACK A BOMB HIT THE WEST END OF THE MAIN BLOCK OF HOUSES. THE BUILDING CAUGHT FIRE AND WAS BURNT OUT. THE WIFE OF THE PRINCIPAL LIGHTHOUSE KEEPER, MRS. MARGARET HELEN SMITH (AGED 60), AND THEIR DAUGHTER MARGARET (GRETA) SMITH (AGED 10) WERE KILLED. A SOLDIER, GUNNER WILLIAM MORRIS (AGED 27) MANNING AN ANTI AIRCRAFT GUN NEARBY WAS ALSO KILLED. EXTENSIVE DAMAGE WAS DONE BY FIRE, BLAST AND FLYING DEBRIS.

MR. RODERICK MACAULAY, ASSISTANT KEEPER AT FAIR ISLE NORTH, WALKED THROUGH SNOW DRIFTS AND GALE FORCE WINDS TO HELP RESTORE THE SOUTH LIGHT. HE RECEIVED THE B.E.M. FOR OUTSTANDING SERVICE.

IN MEMORY OF
MRS. CATHERINE SUTHERLAND
MRS. MARGARET SMITH
MARGARET (GRETA) SMITH
GUNNER WILLIAM G. MORRIS R.A.

THIS PLAQUE IS RAISED
BY
SCOTLANDS LIGHTHOUSE MUSEUM, KINNAIRD HEAD, FRASERBURGH
AND
THE NORTHERN LIGHTHOUSE BOARD

Surrendered U776 at Lerwick in 1945

Shetland Museum

Shetland crofthouse in the later 19th century

Traditionally Shetlanders have been known as *"fishermen with crofts"*, while Orcadians were *"farmers with boats"*, reflecting the relative importance of the sea and the land to the inhabitants. The lack of fertile land in Shetland is more than compensated for by the richness of the marine environment. From the earliest times people relied on fishing, seabirds and sea mammals for food and raw materials.

Since Viking times at least the boats used were clinker-built skiffs or yoles which are very suitable for the sea conditions as well as easy to launch and pull up the beach. Handlines, small nets and creels were all used for inshore fishing. Wooden yoles are still being built today, and can be powered by oars, sail or motor.

Life for crofting families changed little over millennia, and was subject to the vagaries of weather and landlords. Cattle, sheep, pigs, ponies and hens were kept. Barley, oats, kale and latterly potatoes and turnips were grown. While the people had a hard and often insecure life, they also had a very healthy diet and tended to be long-lived.

The growing season in Shetland is short, and in some years crops fail, or the fishing is very poor, leading to great hardship. During the 18th and 19th centuries potatoes became a staple part of the diet, and when blight ruined the crops, starvation faced the people. Many were to emigrate to North America and New Zealand during this time.

The issue of land ownership became important during the 17th and 18th centuries, as more and more Scots arrived and took over land, very often by highly questionable means. Tenants had no security and could be evicted at any time. This became a serious issue with the development of local fisheries and the notorious *"truck"* barter system which gave the landlords virtual total power over their tenants, but also bound the two in a grim need for each other.

The passing of the Truck and Crofters' Acts in the later part of the 19th century did much to help this situation, but the latter also set up the current very complex system of landholding where the landowner has virtually no power, and the crofter has security of tenure. Although they have the right to buy their land, the system of grants makes this unattractive so most crofters remain as tenants.

The 20th century has seen much in the way of agricultural "improvement", some of which is beneficial to production, but part of which is detrimental to the environment. Crofting is by nature a low intensity farming system which works with rather than against nature. The rela-

Shetland yoles at Baltasound, Unst

Modern racing yoles at Walls regatta

tively small number of larger farms have been very successful in supplying local beef and milk, but are restricted to the fertile areas such as Tingwall, Sound, and Dunrossness.

Although agriculture plays only a small part in the economy of Shetland compared to fishing, its importance in maintaining the landscape is quite out of proportion to its monetary value. The mix of cultivated land, pasture and moorland is the result of 5,000 years of man's activities and very much part of what makes Shetland so attractive to people and wildlife.

Shetland Crofthouse Museum (HU397147) at Boddam in the South Mainland is a restored 19th century croft. South Voe was last lived in in 1962, having been built about 1850. With its *but* and *ben* rooms, attached byre, barn and stable, it is not disimilar to the Norse farmsteads of over 1,000 years earlier.

The agricultural landscape is divided into *toun* (infield), separated from the *scattald* (outfield) by a hill-dyke. The *toun* generally consisted of a small group of crofts and was on the better land, being used for growing crops and winter keep, while the animals grazed on the *scattald*, which was common land. In winter the cattle and pigs were taken inside, while sheep and ponies were allowed to graze on toun land. The *scattald* was the source of peats for burning, turves for roofing, rushes and heather for ropes and mould for animal bedding.

Hay-making with coles, Laxo

Runrig strips were used for cultivation and rotation of crops

Planticrub with anti-sheep defences - used for growing vegetables

South Voe, Boddam, Dunrossness - Shetland Crofthouse Museum

Shetland Museum

Shetland Museum

History and Culture

Shetland Ponies at Sumburgh

Bones of ponies the same size as the modern Shetland Pony were found at Jarlshof, dating from perhaps 2,500 years ago or more. Shetland Ponies or *Shelties*, are extremely hardy, and are also very strong for their size. It is unknown if they came with the first settlers, but no doubt they have been used for work and transport since early times.

The ponies' long tails and manes also conveniently provided ideal materials for making fishing lines and nets which were both strong and rot-resistant. they grow long, shaggy, winter coats and doubtless they also were used for many purposes.

Shetland Ponies have short legs, a short back, small ears, but a thick neck and large head. They thrive on a poor diet and can cope with severe weather. They are also very agile and have remarkable stamina. Normally they were kept on the *scattald*, and only taken in when they were needed to work.

Mainly the ponies were used as pack animals to carry home the peats, and all manner of other things. They would also have been used to work the land, but it was only after the building of roads in the 19th century that they were much used for transport.

With the banning of children from working in mines by the Mines Act of 1847, there was suddenly a demand for small, strong ponies which could work in the restricted spaces of the coal mines. This resulted in most of the

Shetland Ponies near Haroldswick, Unst

best stallions being sold south for breeding. Several stud farms were set up, most notably the Londonderry Stud on Noss, to breed ponies for use in the mines and for export to American stud farms.

The foals are very photogenic

There was a fashion in the late 19th and early 20th centuries for children of royalty and the rich to have Shetland Ponies, which meant continuing demand long after mines became mechanised. However, after WWI this market collapsed. The small ponies are now once again in demand, and the breed is promoted by the Shetland Pony Stud Book Society, which was founded in 1890 to *"maintain unimpaired the purity of Shetland Ponies and to promote the breeding of these ponies"*. The main aim was to keep the small size of the ponies, with a maximum height of 42 inches, or 10.2 hands.

They will come and "speak" readily

The market for Shetland Ponies continues to fluctuate, but various schemes to maintain the quality of the local breeding stock, for example by providing regis-tered stallions, or encouraging breeders to keep their best foals, have helped to ensure the future of this unique little horse.

Shetland Ponies can be seen all over the islands, grazing at the side of the road, on moorland, and even eating seaweed on the beaches. They are very friendly and curious, and will pose willingly for the camera. The foals are particularly photogenic. Unst is the stronghold of the pony, but they are kept all over Shetland.

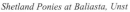

Shetland Ponies at Baliasta, Unst

Shetland Ponies are well-adapted to their environment

There are several agricultural shows

Sheep seem everywhere in Shetland. Most of the hill, or *scattald*, is unfenced and even where there are fences, the sheep are very adept at getting through them. Out of about 400,000 sheep on the islands, less than 100,000 are pure-bred Shetland. The first settlers took Soay sheep with them, and the Vikings took Spaelsau sheep, native to western Norway. The present breed is thus most likely a mixture of the two.

The main and most valuable characteristic of the breed is its exceptionally fine wool. The fleeces are naturally shed in springtime due to a weak point in the fibres which forms in winter, and the *rooing* (plucking) rather than shearing is the traditional method of obtaining the wool.

Shetland sheep are extremely hardy and can survive on a very meagre diet, but they do not thrive in very wet conditions. They are also very agile, as well as long lived, frequently lambing even in their 14th year. Twins are also common. Hill fed lambs are usually about 22kg live weight, and have a very fine

flavoured meat that is very low in fat.

Like North Ronaldsay sheep, Shetland sheep eat seaweed, and it is said that they know when the ebb tide starts. They seem able to sense the change of the tide even when out of sight and sound of the sea. They are also known to predict the weather, and will always take shelter on the lea side of a bank or knoll before the wind starts to blow. They have the ability to shake themselves dry like a dog, unlike other breeds.

There are about eleven main colours of wool, but white is predominant. *Moorit* (brown) and *iset* (grey) are the commonest colours, while black is quite rare. White wool is preferred for dyeing, and the white gene is also dominant.

Since the 18th century and especially in the 20th there has been much cross breeding with Cheviot, Suffolk, Blackface and other types of sheep. Although the result is heavier fleeces, and larger carcasses, the quality of both the wool and the meat is inevitably not so fine.

Traditionally Shetlanders made *reestit* mutton, which is salted and then air-dried. Each family had its own recipe for the pickling solution, and after steeping the joints were hung up in the rafters of the house to dry in peat smoke from the open hearth. The final drying was in *skeos* which are stone built sheds with gaps in the walls to let the wind through.

Sheep awaiting their breakfast at Dales Voe

Clipping time

Peter and Rhoda attending to their sheep

Shetland sheep are very good at getting through fences, but not this one!

Shetland also has its own breed of collie

Shetland sheep are very hardy

SHETLAND RECIPES

REESTIT MUTTON

Ingredients

Joints of mutton, salt, water, a potato. Mix water and salt in a large container. Put the potato into the water and add more salt until the potato floats, then remove it and submerge the mutton in the salt water. Cover and marinade for 3 weeks in a cool place, then hang mutton in a draughty shed to cure and dry.

TATTIE SOUP

Ingredients

1.5l reestit mutton stock
1.5kg potatoes
2 onions
2 carrots
1 turnip (neep - Swede is best)
250g kale (or cabbage)
Put reestit mutton in large pan of cold water, then boil until tender. The stock will be very salty, so dilute to taste. Chop the vegetables and add to the stock., seasoning to taste, and cook gently until the vegetables are tender. Serve with bannocks and sliced *reestit* mutton.

SHETLAND BANNOCKS

Ingredients

125g bere meal, 125g plain flour, 1/2 tsp salt, 1/2 tsp baking powder, 1/2 tsp cream of tartar, 60g butter, buttermilk or milk. Sieve the dry ingredients and rub in butter, moisten with buttermilk to make a soft dough, then knead on a floured board, cut into rounds and bake for 15 minutes at 230C, or until ready.

Fair Isle pattern knitwear

all finely knitted. The fine workmanship of the garments perhaps explains why the Dutch fishermen were so keen on Shetland knitwear.

It was not until the advent of reliable year-round transport that fine woollen goods began to be exported in quantity. These comprised mostly shawls, stockings, underwear, gloves, and caps, and it seems that Queen Victoria was a fan. Shetland knitwear suddenly became fashionable, when favoured by Royalty. Shetland Lace knitwear developed from the 1830s and used the very fine quality of purebred Shetland wool to make uniquely soft garments.

Sheep were present in Shetland from the earliest times, and without doubt their wool was used to make cloth. There is much evidence of spinning and weaving from the Iron Age onwards, but it is unknown when Shetland ladies started knitting. The earliest records refer to a cloth called *wadmel* which was used to make garments and pay rent.

Fine Shetland lace

Knitted gloves, stockings, hats and other items were in great demand by Dutch fishermen who came north every year for the Herring fishery. They were also popular in Germany and Holland and a considerable export trade was built up.

The *"Gunnister Man"*, whose grave was found in 1951 in a peat bank, was clothed in several knitted or woven items, including a jacket, waistcoat, breeches-socks, hat and gloves. All are of a very high quality. Some coins, dating from the 1600s, were in his purse, which was also knitted.

These articles of clothing are the earliest intact examples of knitting or weaving from Shetland. The coat, breeches, shirt and jacket are of woollen cloth, while the gloves, hat and purse were

"Gunnister Man" and his clothes

Spinning by hand

Fine Shetland lace

After WWI there was a revival in the traditional designs which had survived mostly in Fair Isle, and which used naturally dyed wool knitted with several colours in cross and diamond patterns to create brightly coloured jumpers and cardigans.

Following WWII the knitwear industry grew strongly, but remained an essentially home-based activity. Despite ups and downs caused by fashion, and exchange rate fluctuations, genuine Shetland knitwear remains very popular and is exported all over the world. Both traditional and modern designs are produced and are available from many shops and workshops around the islands.

One serious problem has been the adoption of *"Shetland"* as a generic form of knitwear by producers from all over the world. This has been countered to an extent by the **Shetland Knitwear Association** trademark. Another issue is that even though knitted in Shetland, and often by hand, the wool itself is not pure-bred Shetland, but includes that of crossbred fleeces.

Real Shetland wool is the finest and also has more colour variations than any other British breed. The traditional patterns used hand-spun wool, dyed using various plants and natural products. Although modern dyeing methods are mostly used today, many of the designs emulate traditional colour mixes.

HISTORY AND CULTURE

Sullom Voe Oil Terminal was opened in 1978

The discovery of North Sea Oil in the 1970s, and construction of Sullom Voe Oil Terminal, which opened in 1978, led to huge changes in Shetland. After WWII the population continued to decline, and Shetland was clearly in need of an economic miracle. Oil money has led to a great deal of development of roads, harbours, airfields and other infrastructure, as well as leisure centres and investment in businesses.

Although oil throughput has fallen from a peak of over 50 million tonnes per annum to less than 30 million today, it will remain an important part of the economy for some time to come.

Fishing has been greatly expanded and combined with fish farming is now by far the biggest industry in Shetland. Pelagic fish, including Herring and Mackerel, make up the bulk of the catch in tonnage, but white fish, especially Cod and Haddock account for the most value.

The tanker "Braer" went ashore near Sumburgh in 1993

The Shetland fishing fleet has well over 200 modern vessels, ranging in size from the huge Whalsay purse seiners to small inshore boats. The distance from Mainland UK markets means that much of the catch is landed and processed locally, which means that more of the value remains in Shetland. Well over 80,000 tonnes of fish are landed annually.

Salmon Farming began in the early 1980s and has grown to produce over 40,000 tonnes of fish per annum. New developments with other species such as Sea Trout, Halibut and Cod are in development. The clean, cool waters are ideal for these cold water species.

Knitwear was for long the main industry in Shetland, and remains significant with perhaps 1,000 home knitters working part time. The vast

70

majority of production is exported to Asia and Europe where discerning customers want the *"Real Shetland"*.

Agriculture remains a significant player, although dwarfed by fishing, with about 100,000 sheep and 2,000 each of cattle and ponies being exported annually. The trend towards owner-occupation means that less than half the land is now rented, which bodes well for farming. The recent trend to keep more cattle and less sheep can only be good for local producers as well as the environment.

Shetland has always beckoned visitors who are attracted by unspoilt islands, history and wildlife. It will never be a mass market destination, which only adds to its distinctiveness among so many possible choices. Tourism's value to the local economy exceeds knitwear and agriculture combined.

The local economy has diversified with a brewery in Unst and a whisky distillery is proposed.

Most of the larger fishing vessels are based in Whalsay

Sorting nets at Blacksness Pier, Scalloway

Many fishermen work inshore in smaller boats

Salmon cages are a familiar site in many voes

HISTORY AND CULTURE

Burning the galley

Up Helly Aa is held on the last Tuesday of January (*Old Yule*) in Lerwick. There are also similar events in several other parts of Shetland between January and March. This dramatic fire festival developed from an earlier

The Up Helly Aa "Bill"

Shetland tradition of *"guizing"*, or dressing up. Originally straw was used, and the *"skekklers"* traditionally went around the local houses in the countryside at Yule. During the 1800s the young men of Lerwick started to celebrate New Year by burning tar barrels, firing guns and spreading tar on doors and windows. Eventually the authorities stepped in to calm things down.

The phrase *Up Helly Aa* was first used in Lerwick of the festivities of the early 1870s, and the event soon grew in size. The first galley appeared in 1889 and the festival has continued to increase in size and popularity ever since.

Up Helly Aa is run by an organising committee, which is the source of the **Guizer Jarls**. Up

Council reception in the Town Hall in the morning

72

to 1,000 guizers and 49 squads take part in the procession through the street, the burning of the galley and doing their turns in each of 13 halls in the town. Only the Jarl's squad has a Viking theme, and the other squads may choose from politics, local scandal, pop groups, famous people or TV shows.

The event is the culmination of work building the galley and on the costumes and content of each squad's guizing. Although the squads in Lerwick are all-male, the ladies are very much involved in running the halls, and of course in dancing with the guizers in each hall.

The day starts when **"The Bill"** is placed at the Market Cross. The Guizer Jarl proclaims *"Up Helly Aa"* and then follows a series of amusing and often highly satirical anecdotes based on people and events in the last year. Woe betide any local official, politician or other worthy who has appeared in the news. The Bill is signed by the Guizer Jarl with the comment **"We axe for what we want"** - Shetlanders pronounce *"ask"* as *"axe"*.

At 10:00 the Jarl's Squad assemble at the British Legion and after a dram, proceed through the streets with the galley, eventually ending up at the harbour front. Throughout the day the **"Up Helly Aa Song"** is sung, and a red raven banner flies from the Town Hall. After a reception and speeches there the squad then spends the day visiting schools, the hospital and old folks' homes.

The Jarl's Squad pose beside their galley at the pier

Shortly before 19:00 guizers arrive at the muster and form up in four lines, the Guizer Jarl and his squad marches through the ranks to the waiting galley and at 19:00 the lights are extinguished. A maroon goes up, flares are used to light all 1,000 torches, the brass band strikes up with the *"Up Helly Aa Song"* and the Guizer Jarl leads off the procession through the streets of Lerwick.

Thousands of spectators line the streets to watch and after about an hour the galley reaches the burning park, and is surrounded by the

Young Jarl's Squad member

torch-bearing guizers. A maroon is fired and they march around the galley, singing the **"Galley Song"**. The Guizer Jarl then calls for three cheers, a bugle sounds and the torches are thrown into the galley.

The Guizer Jarl leads his squad past the Market Cross

After the light-up, guizers, torches and the galley

Guizers marching in procession

Two members of the Jarl's Squad

Boys' light-up

When the last has been thrown, they all sing *"The Norseman's Home"*.

After the burning some spectators go home, but for many more the night is just beginning as they head for the halls, where festivities last until about 08:00 the next day. Each hall has a host and hostess, who invite the guests and welcome the guizers. Each squad visits every hall in turn, and does a small sketch, which may be amusing, satirical, rude or all three.

Up Helly Aa grew out of Christmas and New Year celebrations which had developed after the Napoleonic Wars, and which by the 1870s had become somewhat rowdy, and were judged not to be in keeping with Lerwick's new refined Victorian image. The new festival of *"Up Helly Aa"* was developed, and gradually took on a Viking theme, which was very much in tune with the times.

By 1906 there was a Guizer Jarl and the festival is now a firmly established part of the Shetland calendar. Although women have never taken part in the Lerwick guizing, families do fully participate in similar events which take place in many other parts of Shetland.

The **Lerwick Galley Shed** has a full-sized replica galley, as well as much memorabilia from previous years' events and is well worth a visit, especially for those who have not been able to attend the real thing.
Up Helly Aa involves a large

Hundreds of guizers circling the galley with their torches

The Raven Banner flying

The guizers throwing their torches into the galley

proportion of the population of Lerwick, and is a genuine community event which lightens up the long dark winter and allows much steam to be vented. The Jarl's Squad is called upon to participate in events in Shetland and elsewhere all year, and presents a *"Viking Shetlander"* image

Children are encouraged to participate early, and there is a junior version, with its own small galley, which is held earlier in the evening. The boys and girls are every bit as keen as their parents, and the junior event is strongly recommended as a prelude to the main procession and burning.

The Guizer Jarl raises his axe with the burning galley behind him

Up Helly Aa Song
Words by J. J. Haldane Burgess
Music by Thomas Manson

From grand old Viking centuries Up Helly Aa has
come,
Then light the torch and form the march, and
sound the rolling drum:
And wake the mighty memories of heroes that are
dumb;
The waves are rolling on.

Chorus

Grand old Vikings ruled upon the ocean vast,
Their brave battle-songs still thunder on the blast;
Their wild war-cry comes a-ringing from the past;
We answer it "A-oi!"
Roll their glory down the ages,
Sons of warriors and sages,
When the fight for Freedom rages,
Be bold and strong as they!

Of yore, our fiery fathers sped upon the Viking
Path;
Of yore, their dreaded dragons braved the ocean in
its wrath;
And we, their sons, are reaping now their glory's
aftermath;
The waves are rolling on.

In distant lands, their raven-flag flew like a
blazing star;
And foreign foemen, trembling, heard their
battle-cry afar;
And they thundered o'er the quaking earth,
those mighty men of war;
The waves are rolling on.

On distant seas, their dragon-prows went
gleaming outward bound,
The storm-clouds were their banners, and their
music ocean's sound;
And we, their sons, go sailing still the wide
earth round and round;
The waves are rolling on.

No more Thor's lurid Hammer flames against
the northern sky;
No more from Odin's shining halls the dark
valkyrior fly;
Before the Light the heathen Night went slow-
ly rolling by;
The waves are rolling on.

We are the sons of mighty sires, whose souls
were staunch and strong;
We sweep upon our serried foes, the hosts of
Hate and Wrong;
The glory of a grander Age has fired our battle-
song;

The Galley Song

Words by John Nicolson
Norwegian Folk Tune

Floats the raven banner o'er us,
Round our Dragon Ship we stand,
Voices joined in gladsome chorus,
Raised aloft the flaming band.

Every guizer has a duty
When he joins the festive throng
Honour, freedom, love and beauty
In the feast, the dance, the song.

Worthy sons of Vikings make us,
Truth be our encircling fire
Shadowy visions backward take us
To the Sea-King's fun'ral pyre.

Bonds of Brotherhood inherit,
O'er strife the curtain draw;
Let our actions breathe the spirit
Of our grand Up Helly Aa'.

The Norseman's Home
("The Hardy Norseman")

Words of unknown origin
Traditional Norwegian Tune

The Norseman's home in days gone by
Was on the rolling sea,
And there his pennon did defy
The foe of Normandy.
Then let us ne'er forget the race,
Who bravely fought and died,
Who never filled a craven's grave,
But ruled the foaming tide.

The noble spirits, bold and free
Too narrow was their land,
They roved the wide expansive sea,
And quelled the Norman band.
Then let us all in harmony,
Give honour to the brave
The noble, hardy, northern men,
Who ruled the stormy wave.

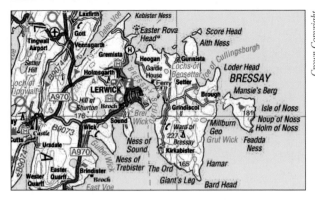

LERWICK (ON *Leir Vik* - Muddy Bay), the bustling main town of Shetland with about 8,000 inhabitants, was founded and grew on fishing, initially by the Dutch, and later by the Scots, English, Russians and others. The town grew from a small cluster of huts where the Shetlanders traded with Dutch fishermen before and during the Herring season.

There was said to be *"great abomination and wickedness committed by the Hollanders and country people"*, and while much drinking and licentious behaviour most likely did occur, there was also a considerable trade in local knitwear, which was much appreciated by the

sailors who in turn brought tobacco, alcohol and fine goods from Holland.

Before any piers were built small *"flitboats"* were used to carry people, goods and supplies to and from ships moored in **Bressay Sound** (ON *Breideyjarsund)*. At first any suitable rocks would have been used, but eventually small jetties were built on the shore below the booths which served as stores, trading places and shore-side accommodation no doubt.

For long the Scots authorities took little interest in events in Shetland, and Lerwick was an excellent place to trade without the inconvenience of paying tax,

until the Customs and Excise finally started to have some influence. Old tunnels and cellars occasionally come to light during building work.

The oldest houses only date from the late 17th century, but several remain from the 18th, when most of the town was clustered between the North and South Ness. The shore was lined by houses, stores and piers which are collectively called **lodberries** (ON *Hlad Berg* - loading rock), most of which have been subsumed by the development of the harbour front.

The 18th century **Lodberry**, at the south end, is one of the most picturesque houses with its thick, battered walls, slipway, pier and fish-drying shed. The **"Peerie Shop"**, which stands on what was Greig's Pier, is several metres from the sea, and surrounded by land, but it was a lodberry.

Commercial Street winds along what was the shore side of the lodberries, and many steep lanes or *"closes"* lead up to Hillhead,

Lerwick from the Ward of Bressay

Lodberry - Lerwick harbour front formerly had many such houses with piers

where the town expanded in the 19th century. The lanes were for long the slums of Lerwick, but many of the remaining houses have now been renovated. The main street has many fine 19th and early 20th century buildings in the style of the period.

Bressay Sound is one of the best natural harbours in Scotland, and was doubtless much used by the Vikings, but they did not establish a settlement or any major buildings. In 1263 King Haakon Haakonson passed through on his major expedition to the west of Scotland which was to lead to failure after the "battle" of Largs on the Clyde.

Although the rocky land was not good for cultivation the wide sheltered harbour with its North and South Mouths was eminently suitable for sailing vessels. Today it is used by many fishing and commercial vessels and is Shetland's principal ferry port. Many yachts also visit in summer. North Sea Oil brought much extra traffic, and continues to do so, while cruise liners find Lerwick a popular destination.

The excellent harbour and the Dutch fleet unfortunately attracted enemy warships during various conflicts. In 1640 several Spanish ships attacked the four Dutch frigates which were there to defend the fleet, and sank two.

In 1653, Cromwell's Admiral Monk was sent with a large fleet to attack the Dutch under Van Tromp. After an inconclusive skirmish during a storm off the west of Shetland, the English landed at Lerwick.

Fort Charlotte was first built about 1665 under Charles II's master mason, John Mylne, during the Dutch Wars, but was attacked and burned by the Dutch in 1673 despite its imposing bastions and gunports. The fort was disused until it was renovated in 1782 and named after the wife of George III. The pentagonal fort was the first substantial building in Lerwick, but today is somewhat lost among the streets and houses which surround it.

In 1792 Arthur Anderson was born in the **Bod of Gremista**, now a museum. He worked with his father in fish curing and drying before joining the Royal Navy in 1808, like many others. He was advised to *"dae weel and persevere"* and did just that. After the Navy he joined a partnership which was to become the Peninsular and Oriental Steam Navigation Co (P&O), which ran the ferry services to Orkney and Shetland until recently.

Anderson made a great deal of money and had the **Anderson Institute** (now Anderson High School) and Anderson Homes (for widows of seamen) built in a grand style. He also served as MP for the Northern Isles for five years, but like all "philantropists" his actions were not entirely altruistic, and when his ideas

Small Boat Harbour

Bod of Gremista interior

The "Dim Riv" is a replica longship which does trips around the harbour

WHAT TO SEE AND DO IN AND AROUND LERWICK

The Lodberry
Bod of Gremista
Shetland Museum
Town Hall
The Knab
Clickimin Broch
Clickimin Centre
Fort Charlotte
Stoney Hill
Bressay - Ward of Bressay
Galley Shed
Up Helly Aa
Lanes
Anderson High School
Commercial Street
Small Boat Harbour
Dim Riv replica longship
Dunter III boat trips
Shopping
Eating Out

Lerwick from Stoneyhill

were not at first fully accepted he left Shetland for good.

Today Lerwick Harbour is a varied hive of activity, with fishing boats, oil-related craft, ferries, cargo boats, yachts and other boats coming and going. Perhaps the most graceful are the *"Shetland Maids"*, the traditional sleek sailing yoles or skiffs. In recent times the old design has been reworked in composite materials rather than wood, and combined with modern sail plans they remain very popular racing boats. Sailing is very popular in Shetland, with weekly points races and annual regattas being held all summer.

Boat trips around the harbour on the replica longship *Dim Riv* are organised in summer, while **Bressaboats** do year-round trips

using a high speed aluminium craft equipped with underwater video. The spectacular Noss cliffs to the east of Lerwick are one of the destinations.

The **Clickimin Leisure Centre** faces its ancient neighbour across the loch and is the result of North Sea Oil money. It says much for the attitude of Shetland Islands Council that they decided to invest in the wellbeing of their voters rather than that of some dubious bank or stock exchange shares. The centre has many facilities, but perhaps the most popular is the leisure pool. Due to its remoteness, Lerwick offers much better shopping facilities than most towns this size. Traditional and modern Shetland knitwear, local jewellery, books and crafts are all available from a variety of inter-

esting shops. Photographers, outdoor enthusiasts of all kinds and people seeking locally produced fish, meat, vegetables and beer are also well catered for.

There is a wide variety of eating places from take aways to *haute*

Norwegian ensign

cuisine. Fresh-caught Haddock and Chips is hard to beat, but beef, lamb, and fish of all other kinds are also very good quality, and many establishments pride themselves with using local produce when they can.

Shetland fiddle music is popular and quite often there are live sessions in bars as well as concerts. The *"Shetland Times"* newspaper is the best place to keep informed about what is on and when.

Lerwick has a useful small library where Internet access is free. It is situated at Lower Hillhead near the Town Hall.

Clickimin Leisure Centre

Commercial Street

Lerwick has lots of steep lanes

LERWICK WALKS

Lerwick's position on a rocky peninsula may not have attracted Neolithic farmers, or even Viking settlers, but its situation does offer a remarkable number of pleasant strolls.

During a walk around the south end there are good view points including from Victoria Pier and the Small Boat Harbour across to Bressay, the Lodberries, and then on to the Knab with views over the *"Sooth Mooth"* and Breiwick. A path continues past the pitch & putt along the coast to Sound and thence back to the centre of town.

The more energetic might try a walk out out past Clickimin Loch, taking in the broch and a walk up to the top of South Stoneyhill, with pleasant views over Lerwick and Bressay. The Clickimin Centre then beckons for its many activities.

Another extension is the fine walk out past the roundabout along Sea Road, eventually ending at the WWII gun emplacements at Sound, from where there is a magnificent view of the *"Sooth Mooth"*.

The map on page 79 covers the centre and environs of Lerwick in detail.

NEW SHETLAND MUSEUM AND ARCHIVES

Shetland Museum and Archives from the ferry

The new Shetland Museum and Archives is built on the historic early 19th century Hay's Dock in Lerwick. It is an inspirational starting point for visitors to Shetland as well as a wonderful new resource for residents.

The Museum tells the "Shetland Story" through a series of twelve zones. The displays are designed to tell this story rather than just present large numbers of artefacts (although over 3,000 are on show).

GALLERIES

LOWER GALLERY

Early Beginnings
Early People
Home and Land
Customs and Folklore
Harvest from the Sea
Boats

UPPER GALLERY

Changing Culture
Trade and Industry
On the Move
Power and State
Maritime and Fisheries
Textiles

The building is innovative and outstanding both in terms of it's expositions and artefacts and as a structure. The design is an icon for Shetland's strong and sustained maritime history and the construction itself is a paradigm, for our times, of eco-sensitivity.

One is struck, in the foyer, by the beautiful and touching re-crafting of objects from Shetland's past into something sustainable for the present and future. The reception desk has been created from the keel of a 19th century German vessel, the *Elenore von Flotow*, whose remains were discovered in Hay's Dock – the original rivets complement the

sensual curves and lines of the aged wood and this is just one example of how organic art forms an intrinsic part of the fittings of the museum and not just items for display.

The flag stone inlays on the floor alongside are a sort of patchwork of Shetland's past and the first impression, therefore, of the Museum and Archives is of an organic, pure and tactile environment.

Naturally, boats are a major feature of the museum. A three storey hall displays several Shetland models hanging in space and also

Boat sheds

includes the last remaining original *sixareen*. The boat sheds are used for the maintenance and restoration of vessels in the collection. Other boats are moored in Hay's Dock.

The building is unique in being both the Museum and Archives. The latter contain records and papers from Shetland's past, dating back to the 15th century as well as a large collection of photographs. Oral history and music archives are also featured. The Archives may be consulted by the public free of charge in a comfortable seachroom.

Additional facilities include the Hay's Dock Cafe Restaurant which has fine views over Lerwick Harbour, especially from its outside seating area. There is also a shop selling local crafts and gifts.

An auditorium which seats 120 people is convenient for conferences and presentations, while there is a temporary exhibition gallery to accommodate art and craft

The boat hall

Shetland Grice - replica of the ancient but now extinct local pig

Inside the Trowie Knowe

displays and items on loan from other institutions.

TROWIE KNOWE

The *Trowie Knowe* is a delightful addition to the museum acknowledging the tradition and existence of folklore and fairy tales within the islands' culture. The ambience within the "Knowe" is vaguely surreal and eerie, with the transient dark shadows and earthy odours and, from the audio installation, the unique and captivating Shetland dialogue of the storytellers completes the sense of being "spirited" away to another world.

Hay's Dock from the cafe/restaurant balcony

CLICKIMIN BROCH AND SETTLEMENT

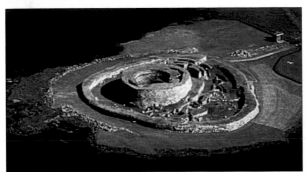

Clickimin Broch aerial view

Bronze Age houses and surrounding massive stone dyke

Interior of the broch showing construction

Blockhouse showing scarcement, stairs and outer wall

CLICKIMIN (ON *klettra minni* - rocky inlet, or perhaps Scots - *"catch them in"*, HU464408) is a settlement site on a small holm on the Loch of Clickimin. It was once joined to the shore by a causeway, when the water level in the loch was higher, making for a good defensive position, but also near the good land of the nearby Ness of Sound. The tidal loch would have been a good place for hauling out boats.

The site was first occupied in the late Bronze Age, about 700BC and a typical small oval house remains from this time. A massive stone dyke was then built around the island, followed by an impressive blockhouse and a broch, which dominates the site today. In the late Iron Age a wheelhouse was built within the broch. Thus, occupation lasted at least 1,000 years.

This interesting but complex site is unusual for Shetland in that of the broch sites so far investigated, most do not have associated domestic buildings or, even more unusually, blockhouses. Occupation ceased well before the arrival of the Vikings, and no evidence of Norse occupation was found.

The blockhouse is built very much in the style of a broch, but as a short curved segment only, with an entrance passage through its centre, and double-skinned walls with in-built cells. It may have served as a symbolic grandiose entrance to the fort, and may also have had wooden structures on the inside face.

The broch is about 20m in diameter and still up to 5m high in places, with a central space 10m in diameter. It may originally have been up to 15m high. The whole site is most impressive, but because of the various excavations and repair by 19th century gentlemen of Lerwick, it is hard to know what is original, and thus hard to understand.

This in no way takes away from the feeling of timelessness that one gets from a visit, especially when one ponders that Greeks, Romans, Picts and Vikings all came in earlier times. It is well worth buying the guide and taking time to study the ruins with its help. Although some of the conclusions from the 1950s excavation may be challenged today, the site remains one of the most interesting in Shetland.

Blockhouse and broch from entrance passage

Clickimin Broch floodlit

BRESSAY & NOSS

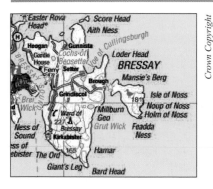

Kirkabister Ness lighthouse with wrecked Russian trawler

BRESSAY (ON *Breidey - breidr*, broad) forms the east side of Lerwick Harbour - an old saying *"Amsterdam waas biggit oot o' da back o'Bressa"*, refers to the importance of the harbour to Dutch fishermen. Bressay remains important to the fishing with its very large *Shetland Catch* processing factory which handles much of the pelagic fish caught in Shetland waters.

The Old Red Sandstone rocks of Bressay and Noss give them a different aspect to most of Shetland, with rounded hills, and fertile soils in places, fringed by a rocky cost, with high cliffs at the Ord (HU497368, 150m) and the Bard. The sandstone beds quarry easily and Bressay stone from **Aith Ness** in the north of the island was much used for building in former times.

Bressay is only a few minutes' ferry ride from Lerwick and makes a good first island visit. To the south, the lighthouse at **Kirkabister Ness** was built by the Stevensons in 1858, and has its very own natural arch. There is a spectacular panoramic view from **The Ward** (HU503388, 226m), which has a convenient road to the summit.

St Mary's Church at Cullingsburgh in the north (HU522422) dates originally from the 10th century, though the "transepts" are 17th century. In the graveyard there is an interesting tombstone to the Captain of a Dutch East Indiaman dated 1636, and the *Bressay Stone* was found here. The church is clearly built from the adjacent broch. The nearby voe is also an excellent place to view wildlife, such as Gannets, Otters and Seals.

Bressay Sound from the Ward of Bressay (226m)

St Mary's Church, Cullingsburgh, Bressay

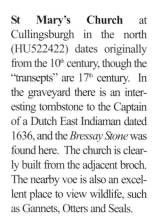

Heading east over to Noss there is a Bronze Age burnt mound with *souterrain* at Wadbister, and a spectacularly sited broch overlooks Noss Sound at the end of the road. There are good walks from here, both north to Ander Hill with its WWI lookout, and south to the Bard and the Ord.

Kirkabister Ness lighthouse with NorthLink ferry "Hjaltland" passing

However, by far the best way to appreciate the Bressay cliffs with their caves and natural arches is by taking one of the boat trips from Lerwick, which offer spectacular close-up views.

With its fertile soil, Bressay was clearly favoured by Bronze Age and Iron Age people, who left many burnt mounds and ruined brochs in evidence. Today the island remains attractive to visitors and locals alike. One place not to miss is **Maryfield House**, a *Restaurant with Rooms*, which offers a wide variety of seafood and other dishes - but phone to book (01595 820207).

Orkneyman's Cave - Seal Cave, Bressay

Giant's Leg, Bard Head, Bressay

BRESSAY AND NOSS

The Noup of Noss (181m) and Rumble Wick from the south

It is interesting that no broch has been found on Noss, but there are at least three nearby on Bressay, with one particularly imposing ruin guarding Noss Sound, another at Brough covering the landward approach and yet another over the hill at Cullingsburgh beside St Mary's Kirk.

This charming little island is one of the best places in Shetland for good views of breeding seabirds, which can be watched without disturbance from the clifftops. In summer there is a small ferry which runs across Noss Sound from Bressay which is run by Scottish Natural Heritage (SNH). Trips from Lerwick by *Bressaboats* allow wonderful views of the cliffs from seaward and are much recommended. Porpoises *(Neesicks)* and seals *(selkies)* are often seen in the Sound of Noss.

In summer Noss is also particularly good for wild flowers, partly because the sheep are kept off the moorland in the bird breeding season, which allows plants

NOSS (ON *Nos* - nose or point of rock), off the east side of Bressay, is a National Nature Reserve. In summer the sandstone ledges of the eastern cliffs are host to huge numbers of breeding seabirds including 45,000 pairs of Guillemots, 7,000 pairs of Gannets, 6,000 pairs of Fulmars, 3,000 pairs of Kittiwakes as well as Puffins, Shags, Razorbills, and Black Guillemots. Herring and Great black-backed Gulls, Great and Arctic Skuas also breed inland. Gannets and Fulmars only started breeding here about 1900, and Great Skua in 1914.

Above the landing place are the ruins of an ancient church, which may have had a round tower, and its graveyard, beside the 17th century farm, now a visitor centre. The nearby pony pund was built to stable Shetland pony mares, when the island was used to breed ponies to work in coal mines in the late 19th century.

Watching an underwater camera

Gannet in flight

Gannets breed on the Noss cliffs

which might otherwise be eaten to flourish, and partly due to the fertility of the Old Red Sandstone soils. The richest vegetation is anywhere where the sheep cannot reach, especially the upper cliff slopes.

During the late 19th century the Marquis of Londonderry leased the island to rear Shetland ponies for use in his coalmines. Prior to this Noss was said to have produced the best milk in Shetland. **Cradle Holm** was joined to Noss by a ropeway which could transport a man and a sheep to the stack. It was, however, judged unsafe and removed in the 1860s.

The Noup of Noss (181m) from below

Holm of Noss or Cradle Holm

Noss seen from the Whalsay ferry

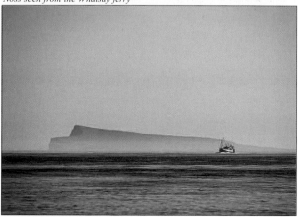

SCALLOWAY

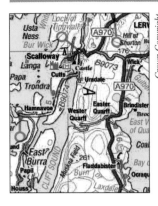

Scalloway from Port Arthur

SCALLOWAY (ON *Skali Vagr* - Longhouse Bay) in 1665 had *"about 100 poor houses and a pretty stone house of the King's where the Governor resides"*. The former Shetland capital is well-sheltered from the Atlantic and at the southern end of Tingwall Valley, less than 3 miles from Law Ting Holm and old St Magnus Kirk.

On the west side and near the fertile Tingwall Valley, with some of the best land in Shetland, Scalloway was the obvious place for settlers to beach their ships and eventually establish a village. There was a substantial broch and settlement here in Iron Age times which was occupied from 100BC or before. The site was found during clearance for construction work, and nothing can be seen today.

The broch was in use for about 600 years, and was destroyed by an intense fire. Large quantities of carbonised grain were found on excavation. Further artefacts indicated connections with other parts of Britain.

The view over Scalloway from the Lerwick road is one of the best in Shetland, with the village, East Voe and in the background many small islands. A short walk southwards along the crest of Easterhoull yields an even better panorama, while a stroll along the street and around the harbour is always interesting.

The bastard son of King James IV, Robert Stewart, became Earl of Orkney and Shetland in the late 1500s. His rule was corrupt and he worked with complete disregard for local laws and tra-

Aerial view of Scalloway from the east

tions. Through this he and his Scottish collaborators acquired much land and property by highly dubious means. His son Patrick was no better, but he was executed for treason - not extortion and theft - in 1615.

For Shetland the ultimate was the building of Scalloway Castle at the expense of the local people about 1599. In use for only a very short time, this incongruous ruin still dominates the village despite all the pier-building of recent times. Today its malevolent presence is quite diminished by the nearby industrial estate and by the **North Atlantic Fisheries College** at Port Arthur, a strong portent of Shetland's future.

Da Haaf Restaurant, at the main North Atlantic Fisheries College building, is open daily. It specialises in the best of Shetland's seafood, fresh from the local markets. The menu includes Halibut, Lemon Sole, Turbot, Plaice, Salmon and Trout.

As Lerwick developed, so Scalloway declined, but during the 19th century many fishing smacks worked out of the village, and today fishing is the mainstay of the economy. A large wharfage area at Blackness provides facilities for fishing and cargo boats, and many fishing vessels operate from here.

In winter the harbour area is a good place to look for birds such as Glaucous, Iceland and Ring-billed Gulls.

During WWII the *"Shetland Bus"* was based here from 1942 to 1945 and operated many clandestine missions to Norway, carrying men, munitions and equipment. The *Prince Olav slipway* was built to repair the boats used. This operation and other aspects of Scalloway's history are well-documented in the Scalloway Museum.

Stewart coat of arms on Castle

Shetland Bus memorial, unveiled June 2003

Scalloway from the east

BURRA ISLE AND TRONDRA

Aerial view of Hamnavoe and Burra Isle from the north west

TRONDRA (ON *Thrandrey* - Thrandr's Island) is joined to the Mainland by a bridge. Burland is named for a now disappeared broch. There are very fine views

Papil cross-slab

Shetland Museum

from here over towards the West Mainland and the small islands of Hildasay, Papa and Oxna.

Another bridge joins **BURRA ISLE** (*Borgarey* - Broch Island) to Trondra with its pretty village of **Hamnavoe** (ON *Hafnarvagr* - Harbour Bay), which has grown a lot since 1890 when there were only six cottages here. In the early part of the 20th century several streets of fishermen's cottages were built, which have traditionally been painted with left-over boat paint.

With its moored small fishing boats, both old and new, dinghies hauled up, fishing gear, narrow lanes, pretty gardens and quaint cottages Hamnavoe is something of a photographer's or artist's paradise. Today most of the larger boats are based in Scalloway.

The *Burra Haaf* lies close enough inshore to allow the use of *fourareens*, each with a four man crew, rather than the larger *sixareens* used for the offshore *Haaf* fishing. The picture oppo-

Hamnavoe has a very sheltered harbour

site was taken in the early 20ᵗʰ century and shows the yoles pulled up into their nousts behind the bod. The fish were spread out to dry on the stoney part of the beach, while the small building is the ice house, in which ice from the loch was stored, for preserving fish. Bait was obtained from Gloup Voe and Basta Voe.

Larger decked sailing smacks replaced the *fourareens* in the early 1900s, and the deep, sheltered harbour at Hamnavoe was ideal for them, while the location was convenient for all the grounds to the west.

Burra Isle has some of the best beaches in Shetland where the hardy can swim, and others just stroll, notably those at **Meal**, **Banna Minn** and **West Voe**. There are pleasant walks to the remote Kettla Ness and Houss Ness where otters and seals may be seen. There are lovely views towards the West side of the South Mainland from here.

Papil (ON *Papabol* - Priest's Farm) is one of the main ancient Church sites in Shetland, and the name shows that there was a well-established Christian community here well before the Vikings arrived. The name *papar* is used to refer to both Puffins and priests in Iceland still today.

Unfortunately the **Cross Kirk** here was demolished in 1790 to build the current small church. The original building is thought to have had a tall, round tower, similar to that at Egilsay in Orkney.

Meal - lovely beach near Hamnavoe

Brough, looking along the beach to Ness of Papil, Loch of Papil at right.

Shetland Museum

The **Papil cross-slab** as well as the **Monks' Stone** and other parts of an altar shrine were found in the graveyard here, and their style suggests connections with the Pictish rather than the Columban tradition in Scotland. Both may date from the 8ᵗʰ century. It has been suggested that the Monks' Stone may commemorate the arrival of Christian priests on Burra Isle.

Banna Minn at the south end of West Burra Isle

SOUTH MAINLAND

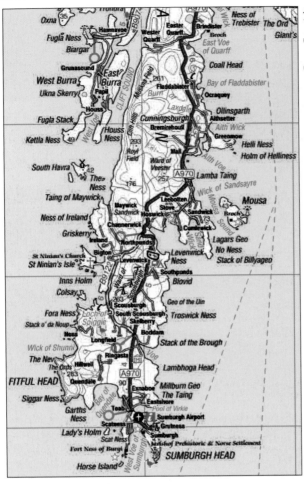

down the peninsula, ending at the dramatic **Fitful Head** (ON *Viti fjall* - Ward Hill, (HU347137, 283m) on the west and Sumburgh Head with its lighthouse in the east.

The road runs south from Lerwick past **Gulberwick** (ON *Gulberruvik* - Gulberra's Wick) and the Loch of Brindister with its small dun. There are nearly always friendly Shetland Ponies here, and often birds on the loch. Easter Quarff (ON *Hvarf* - turning point), has fine views over green fields to the east, while pretty Wester Quarff overlooks Clift Sound and Burra Isle.

The **Broch of Burland** (HU 446361) is dramatically sited in an isolated position on a headland above the Wick of Burland. There is a whole string of brochs lining the coast of the South Mainland, mostly in similar vantage points, but this is one of the most spectacular.

Outcrops of limestone were quarried at **Fladdabister** (ON *Flatibolstadir* - Flat Farm, HU437321) in the 19th century and lime was made in peat-burning kilns. At **Catpund** (ON *Kot Pund* - Cottage Enclosure, or *Catt*, referring to the (Pictish) tribe HU423270), south of Cunningsburgh, there is a large outcrop of *steatite*, or soapstone, which was used from Neolithic times to make pots, plates and bowls. The soft rock is easily worked, but when tempered by heat becomes quite strong and fire-resistant. It was used in large quantities by the Vikings.

The **SOUTH MAINLAND** stretches like the blade of a sword over 20 miles southwards from Lerwick, but is never more than a few miles wide. A spine of hills runs most of the way

Gulberwick, south of Lerwick

Cunningsburgh from the south with Bressay in the background

Cunningsburgh (ON *Konungs Borg* - King's Broch) is another fertile crofting township with burnt mounds, a broch and an ancient cemetery where a carved cross-slab, and several other inscribed stones have been found. Aith Voe is especially attractive, with its moored small boats.

Burraland broch, Sandwick, overlooking Mousa Sound

A walk to tranquil **Helli Ness** (ON *Helli Ness* - Flat Rock Point) is really worthwhile and may well be rewarded by an Otter sighting. **Aith Voe** is also a prime site to watch out for waders during the migration season. The pretty crofthouse of Mail, with its nearby meadows ablaze with wild flowers in summer, especially Primroses in May, makes a pleasant viewpoint.

Primroses at Mail

Steatite workings at Catpund

Shetland yole at Aith Voe, Voxter, Cunningsburgh

97

Mousa Broch is on the west side of the little island of Mousa

Mousa broch is smaller in diameter than most, and today there is no sign of any surrounding structures apart from a possible rampart. Across the sound its neighbour, Burraland broch, does have evidence of settlement around it, but awaits further investigation.

Many visitors to this attractive little island go no further than its broch, but there are many further delights in store, including within the broch itself a large colony of Storm Petrel *(Alamootie)* which find the interstices in the walls ideal for nesting. During the day they can be glimpsed through cracks, but during the short hours of summer darkness they fly in with food and to exchange brooding with their mates.

MOUSA (ON *Mos-ey* - Mossy Island) lies across Mousa Sound from Sandwick, and is the site of the famous and very well-preserved eponymous broch, which was already at least 1,000 years old in Viking times. This impressive, yet stark structure is built from local sandstone to a very high standard, which no doubt has ensured its survival. The smooth exterior is "battered" so that the bottom diameter is 15m but the top only 12m.

The interior is about 6m across with a later wheelhouse complicating interpretation. There are three intramural cells at ground level, and the entrance passage is about 5m long. There are two scarcements to support wooden floors, one about 2m above the other, and a series of spaces which no doubt lightened the structure.

Above the first level, the walls are hollow, with lintels joining them and making a series of stairs and landings to access higher floors and the top of the broch, over 13m above ground level.

Mousa is also a very good place to observe seals. There is a large colony of Common Seals which haul out at the south end, especially in the West and East Pools. Their young are born in June and July, while the Grey Seals, which may also be seen here, have their young in Autumn.

Stairs lead to the top of the broch

The interior showing scarcement

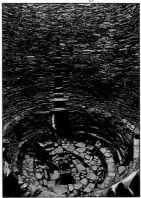

Porpoises *(Neesick)* are frequently seen in Mousa Sound, while other cetaceans such as Killer Whales, Dolphins and Minke Whales are also sometimes seen. All are attracted by the massive shoals of Sandeels which congregate here in summer. Skuas, Gulls, Terns, Eider Duck and Black Guillemot all nest here, while the small lochs and the Pools are good places to see waders.

Mousa and Mousa Sound from the Broch of Burraland

Burnt mounds, a prehistoric house, a Norse mill and and the more recent *Haa'* attest to earlier inhabitants, but the real colour is added by two mentions in the Norse Sagas. *Egil's Saga* tells of a young man from Sognefiord who was in love with a girl called Thora. She insisted on accompanying him on a Viking trip to Dublin, but they were wrecked on Mousa, where they spent the winter in the broch, before departing to Iceland where she gave birth to a daughter called Asgerd.

The *Orkneyinga Saga* tells of the beautiful Margaret, who on the death of her husband Earl Maddad, went off with Gunni,

The structure is mostly probably original, but repairs were done in the 1800s

brother of Sweyn Asleifson, to whom she bore a child. However Erlend *Ungi* (the Young) soon took her fancy and they made off and settled into *Moseyjarborg*. Her son Earl Harald Maddadson was enraged by her behaviour, but despite besieging the broch he found it *"a hard place to get at"*. Eventually mother and son were reconciled when he agreed to let her marry Erlend in return for his

support in his Earldom disputes. Whether eloping lovers would find Mousa broch a cosy love-nest nowadays is perhaps doubtful, but it is still nice to imagine these Viking antics of 1,000 years ago when visiting this lovely little island. Even on the wildest of days it is tranquil inside the broch, which with a roof and a roaring peat fire must have been quite cosy, if perhaps a little smelly for modern noses.

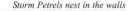

Storm Petrels nest in the walls

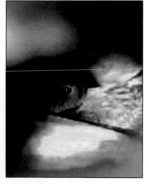

Tom Jamieson operates daily trips to Mousa in the season

The beautiful ayre joining St Ninian's Isle to the Mainland

ST NINIAN'S ISLE (ON *Rinansey*) is joined to the Mainland at Bigton by a long and beautiful sandy *ayre* or *tombolo*. The views are some of the most stunning in Shetland, while the constantly changing light only adds to the impact of the scene.

The **St Ninian's Chapel** (HU368209) dates from the 12th century, but overlies a much older, possibly 8th century one, which was the site of the discovery in 1958 of the *"St Ninian's Isle Treasure"*. Ninian was a 5th century Celtic saint who is mentioned by Bede as having converted the southern Picts. Whether the earlier chapel was dedicated to him is not clear.

During excavation in 1958, Shetland schoolboy Douglas Coutts discovered a Larch box which contained 28 Pictish silver items (plus part of a Porpoise jaw). The box was covered by a stone with an incised Celtic cross.

All of the treasure is currently in the National Museum in Edinburgh, as a Court case at the time ruled that it belonged to the Crown, over-ruling *Udal Law*. Replicas are on display in Shetland Museum and Archives in Lerwick. The collection includes 12 brooches, several bowls, and a hanging lamp which date from about 800AD.

Also found were a number of carved stones, including an 11th century steatite hog-back tombstone, several altar corner-pieces like those from Papil and a number of Christian grave-markers. There is also a holy well nearby (HU367207). Many of these items are in the Shetland Museum.

Aerial view of St Ninian's Isle from the south east

Visitors should not miss the walk around the island. There are dramatic views northwards to Walls, westwards to Foula and southwards to Fitful Head, while the coast has low cliffs with many caves, small geos and a natural arch.

In summer the scene is enlivened by many wild flowers, while in a winter storm the seas break dramatically over the cliffs. Seals haul out on the rocks, and with luck an Otter may be seen fishing in the ebb. St Ninian's Isle is an *essential visit* at any time of year and is normally accessible except at unusually high tides.

Replicas of the Pictish silver and real altar stones in the Shetland Museum

Looking across to St Ninian's Isle from the Bigton side

Sumburgh Head lighthouse is the oldest in Shetland

Sumburgh Head (ON *Sunnborg* - South Broch, after the broch which stood where the lighthouse is now), is one of the best places to get close-up views of Puffins and other seabirds in summer. Humpback, Killer, Minke and other whales also regularly turn up. The lighthouse was built by Robert Stevenson in 1821, and the RSPB office now occupies one of the keepers' houses. The headland itself is one of several RSPB reserves in Shetland.

The Sumburgh area is one of the best in Shetland for birders with its lochs including **Spiggie Loch** (another RSPB Reserve), **Loch of Hillwell**, **Loch of Brow** and **Loch of Clumlie**. The **Pool of Virkie** is especially attractive to waders, while the garden at the **Sumburgh Hotel** is a good place to look for passerines during migration. There are many suitable vantage points from which the car makes a good hide.

There are several pleasant walking opportunities at the *"sooth end"*. The energetic may try the stiff climb up to the top of **Fitful Head** (HU346137, 283m), with its panoramic views and dramatic cliffs - but watch out for fog, as

DUNROSSNESS (ON *Dynrost* - noisy strong tide, from the roar of the Sumburgh Roost) is the parish name for the South Mainland. Tidal streams from east and west meet here and, even on a calm day, there can be overfalls which are dangerous for small boats. The mixing makes for plenty of food for fish, and the shoals in turn attract seabirds and cetaceans.

Humpback Whales are seen off Sumburgh in summer

Puffin - Tammy Norie - at Sumburgh Head

all too often it has a "hat" on. The top can be reached via a track from Hillwell, or as part of a longer circular walk taking in Noss Hill with its WWII radar site, and the clifftops, perhaps returning via Garth's Ness, the site of the loss of the tanker *Braer,* in 1993.

Waves breaking at West Voe of Sumburgh

Both Scatness and Sumburgh Head make interesting circular walks. There is an excavated but enigmatic Iron Age blockhouse on the **Ness of Burgi** (HU387084) which is protected by two ditches and ramparts. A similar but more ruinous structure lies just to the north. The **Loch of Gards** is a good place to find waterfowl and waders.

Beach lovers are also well catered for with spectacular sandy bays at West Voe of

Sumburgh Head from the east

SOUTH MAINLAND

Colsay and Spiggie Loch with Sumburgh Head in the background

Quendale Mill (HU372133) was built in 1867 and has been fully restored to working order. It is one of three large 19th century watermills in Shetland, the others being at Girlsta and Weisdale. The Quendale (ON *Kverndalr* - Mill Dale) area has some of Shetland's best land, and the dairy farms here supply much of Shetland's milk.

The mill served the Quendale Estate as well as crofts and farms in the South Mainland until it ceased operating in 1948. There are displays of old farm machinery and photographs as well as an interesting craft shop.

Sumburgh, Bay of Quendale and Scousburgh. More intimate are Spiggie Beach, Grutness Voe and Rerwick. The Links of Quendale make up the largest machair area in Shetland, and are a riot of colour in summer.

Dunrossness was settled early, and there are several archaeological sites on the *must visit* list, including **Jarlshof** and **Old Scatness Broch**, both of which were occupied for thousands of years and preserved under sand dunes.

There are a remarkable number of brochs in this area, all of which are worth a visit. At Eastshore near the Virkie Marina the broch is being eroded by the sea, while there are broch mounds at Broken

Brough (HU407129), Dalsetter (HU408157) and Lunabister (HU378165). The Dalsetter broch is surrounded by a deep ditch and rampart which encloses a settlement site, while the one at Lunabister has fine views over Spiggie Loch.

The **Crofthouse Museum** at South Voe, Boddam is a restored mid-19th century croft. It was built about 1850 and last occupied in 1962. The house has a *but* and a *ben* end, while the byre is on the down-slope end, and the barn with kiln is set on the rear. The whole is not dissimilar in layout to Norse houses from 1,000 years earlier. Within a small area Shetland's history from the Bronze Age to the 20th century can be traced.

Dalsetter broch

Eastshore broch

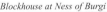

Blockhouse at Ness of Burgi

Old Scatness settlement site under excavation

Quendale Water Mill - restored workings

Crofthouse Museum with barn, byre and kiln

Crofthouse Museum - "ben" end interior

16ᵗʰ century "Auld Hoose O'Sumburgh" with Norse houses in foreground

The name **Jarlshof** was coined by the Scottish novelist, Walter Scott, when he visited in 1815, but the present settlement site was only revealed after a big storm years later. From the 1890s until the 1950s the site was cleared out and excavated.

The remains are complex and many layered through millennia of occupation, and thus rather hard to interpret. A substantial part of it has also been lost to the sea. The oldest visible walling , in the north east corner, dates from before 2500BC, while pottery like that from Skara Brae in Orkney was found here indicating that the earliest settlers may have been here.

There are several ovoid houses in front of the museum which are Bronze Age, two of which have *souterrains*. With their internal walls which subdivide the houses into cells, these houses are typical of Shetland dwellings of the time. One was later used around 800BC as a smithy to cast bronze tools, arms and decorative items using clay moulds.

Later, in the Iron Age, further small round houses were built nearer the shore. The substantial broch survives to about 2.4m high, though most of it has been used as a convenient quarry for later buildings or lost to the sea. The broch may date from about 200BC.

A number of *"wheelhouses"* are built in a cluster in and around the broch. This distinc-

tive type of structure is also found at Old Scatness, and in the Western Isles. The circular houses have radial stone *"spokes"* which divide the living space and would have helped support the roof. When there is a space between the piers and the walls the houses are described as *"aisled"*.

Evidence of Pictish influence in the form of painted quartz stones, and distinctive designs carved on stones was found. The wheelhouse complex continued to be inhabited for a few hundred years, but it is not clear if the site was occupied when the Vikings arrived around 800AD.

Carved stone

The large complex of ruins to the north west of the broch represents several centuries of settlement dating from the 9ᵗʰ to the 14ᵗʰ centuries. The original house was over 20m long, with outhouses and a possible bath house. Construction was stone and turf walls, with wooden roof supports and perhaps interior wall linings. Benches lined the walls and there was a large central hearth.

Over the centuries extensions,

Bronze moulds, axe head and sword from approx 800BC

alterations and new building combined with clearing out in a manner that did not take stratigraphy very seriously, has resulted in a fascinating but puzzling maze of walls, paths and paved areas.

This only adds to the interest, and makes one wonder what else may lie beneath the sand. Later buildings include a medieval farm, part of which was removed to reveal the Bronze Age houses. Robert Stewart renovated the house in the late 16th century, while his son Patrick had a further extension built about 1605, and it was this, the present ruined house, or *"Auld Hoose O'Sumburgh"* that Scott called *"Jarlshof"*.

Norse period paved path

Intricately carved bone

Norse longhouse showing walls, hearth, benches and entrance

Wheelhouse interior

JARLSHOF CHRONOLOGY

2500BC	oldest pottery
2000BC	oldest house
700BC	bronze smiddy
500BC	souterrains built?
200BC	broch built
100BC	aisled wheelhouse
AD	
after 800	Norse settlement
1400s	medieval farmhouse
1590	Robert Stewart
c.1605	Patrick Stewart
1700s	abandoned
1814	Walter Scott visits
1920s	sand cleared out
1950s	excavated

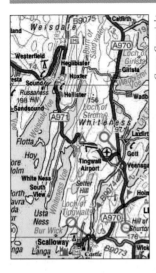

Crown Copyright

The "Murder Stone"

TINGWALL (ON *Thingvollr* - where the Althing was held) is an attractive and fertile valley north of Scalloway. The farmland, golf course, loch and landscape make it different to most of Shetland. The **Law Ting Holm**, where assizes were held, is at the north end of the loch and is joined to the shore by a causeway. The old St Magnus Church, seat of the Archdeacon, with its tall tower, stood nearby until the late 18th century, when it was demolished.

Throughout Norse times Tingwall was thus the centre of both secular and ecclesiastic power, while nearby Scalloway was the main port and later the administrative centre until the development of Lerwick in the 18th and 19th centuries.

The mysterious **"Murder Stone"** (HU412420) is said to mark the place where in 1389 *"Malise Sperra was slain with seven others by the Earl of Orkney"*. Malise, Lord of Strathearn, became the first of the Sinclair Earls of Orkney about 1336 and was succeeded in 1379 by his nephew Henry Sinclair - the very last "Viking"

Earl. Malise Sperra was his cousin and the fight in 1389 was all about Henry gaining control in Shetland.

The **Asta Golf Course** is compact but picturesque and challenging, while anglers enjoy a different challenge on Asta and Tingwall Lochs. Ducks, waders and swans breed here, and the marshy shorelines are full of wildflowers in summer. The lochs are also good places to seek migrants and winter visitors, the car making an excellent hide. Oystercatchers obligingly pose as they nest at the roadside.

WHITENESS (ON *Hvitanes* - White Ness) gets its name and the greenness of its vegetation from the limestone which outcrops in the area. There is a panoramic view from **Wormadale** (HU404463) and a convenient car park from which a short walk south along the ridge leads to a chambered cairn at the summit of **Nesbister Hill** - and an even better view. In the opposite direction, on the south ridge of **Wormadale Hill** (HU405466, 140m) is a 2.5m high standing stone.

A ruined broch is unusually situated on **Barra Holm** (HU387458) in Stromness Voe about 60m from the shore and was reached by a causeway at low tide. **Loch of Strom** (ON *Straumr* - tidal flow, stream) has a small medieval castle on an island near the south end, while the bridge with its strong tidal flows is a good place to catch Sea Trout in season.

Loch of Tingwall from the Law Ting Holm

WEISDALE (ON *Vissadal - Vissa* is the old name of the Weisdale Burn) has the only substantial woodland in Shetland at Kergord, near the restored **Weisdale Mill**, home to the Bonhoga Art Gallery and its excellent cafe. The programme includes visual and applied art as well as touring exhibitions throughout Shetland.

There are expansive views southwards from Scord of Sound (HU380506), while the energetic will find even grander vistas from the top of Hill of Sound, easily reached by a track. The ridge walk along the West Hill of Weisdale to Scalla Field (HU390572, 281m) will yield further panoramic views and in summer many moorland species of birds breed here including Curlew and Whimbrel.

Aerial view of Weisdale Voe from the north

Whiteness Voe from Wormadale - spring snow

Kergord Woods, Weisdale

Chambered Cairn on Nesbister Hill

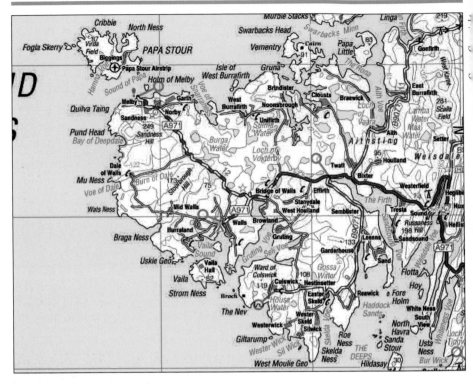

"DA WASTSIDE" is the peninsula which reaches out into the Atlantic from Weisdale in the south to Voe in the north. It includes Aithsting, Walls and Sandness and is remarkable for its scenery and its wealth of archeological remains.

Most of the area is formed from Old Red Sandstone, which yields fertile soils, but also is easily eroded by the sea, leading to extensive firths and voes which penetrate far into the land, especially in Walls and Bixter. However, gneiss on the north

coast and granite on the south east coast have also afforded some protection from erosion. This has resulted in dramatic cliff scenery in several places, especially in the Skeld and Deepdale areas.

The numerous lochs provide excitement for the angler and habitat for breeding birds, while the heavily indented shore with many small burns is ideal territory for the elusive Otter. The sheltered voes are also very good places to observe migrating and wintering wildfowl and waders.

Aurora Borealis from Twatt, Bixter

TRESTA (ON *Trestadir* - Tree Farm?) is one of the few places in Shetland where trees will grow. This pretty, fertile, south-

Vementry

Sunset over Aith Voe

facing township faces land-locked Tresta Voe, which extends into The Firth and Bixter Voe and reaches the open sea via Sandsound Voe.

BIXTER (ON *Byggsetr* from *bygg* - barley) and **Twatt** (ON *Thweit* - clearing among rocks) form another fertile area which reaches to Clousta in the north west and Aith in the north. There is a well-preserved chambered cairn with a fine view at **Park Hall** (HU312529) and an unusual inland broch at Houlland (HU345539).

AITH (ON *Eid* - isthmus) takes its name from the broad isthmus separating Walls from the rest of the Mainland. It is the base for the Westside RNLI lifeboat. The sheltered Aith Voe leads to **Swarbacks Minn**, where the Royal Navy Cruiser Squadron was based in WWI. The drive from Aith to Voe is especially scenic, with new views around every corner. East Burrafirth and Gonfirth are two of the *"must stop and look"* places.

VEMENTRY (ON *Vemundarey* - Vemundr's Isle) is a small island at the north end of Aith Ness. Apart from one of

the best preserved chambered cairns in Shetland, overlooking Northra Voe (HU290512), it also has poignant reminders of the 20th century in the form of abandoned naval 6in guns on the Muckle Ward. There are interesting views from here over Swarbacks Minn to Muckle Roe and Northmavine and to Foula.

Voe of Clousta is one of many scenic indentations in the Westside coastline

Chambered cairn at Park Hall, overlooking Effirth and Bixter Voes

Reawick takes its name from the red granite sands

SKELD (ON *skjoldr* - shield), **SAND** and **REAWICK** (ON *ryodr* - red) are thriving communities on the southern part of the Westside peninsula. The hard rock has led to spectacular low cliffs, stacks and pretty coves at **Silwick**, **Westerwick** and **Culswick**.

There are many prehistoric sites worth visiting, including chambered cairns, houses, field systems and brochs. The **Stanydale** transepted house or "Temple" (HU285502) and associated houses is one, and the ruined broch at **Culswick** in its spectacular location (HU254448), is another. The 12th century chapel at **Sand** (HU347473) also merits a visit.

Gruting Voe with its extensions at Seli Voe, Scutta Voe and Voe of Browland reaches in past the Bridge of Walls. All of this area is good for seabirds, moorland birds and Otters, and there are many prehistoric remains, most of which only become apparent once *"one gets one's eye in."*

WAAS (ON *Vagar* - sheltered bays), or Walls as the mapmakers would have it, forms the mostly low and in places fertile western extremity. It is also host to some of Shetland's most spectacular Neolithic monuments at **Scord of Brouster** (HU258516) and at **Pinhoulland** (HU260498) as well as many chambered cairns and burnt mounds.

There are several ruined brochs in the area, including one well inland at Brough, which must signify the importance of Walls 2,000 years ago. There are wonderful views west to Foula from many places, but perhaps the best is from **Swinister** (HU178511), overlooking the broch on the Loch of Watsness.

One of the finest walks in Shetland goes from Dale (HU180527) in the north of Walls to Huxter (HU174574) in Sandness. The low cliffs have many caves and sheltered bays. Seals seem to favour Seli Ayre.

The Burn of Deepdale is indeed deep, but the steep climb afterwards is worth the view over the

Silwick

Walls from the west

Bay of Deepdale with its 170m high eroding banks and shingle beach. There are fine views towards Papa Stour from the top of Sandness Hill (HU192558, 249m).

VAILA (ON *Vala-ey* - Vali's Isle) is an attractive small island south of Walls with a large *Haa'* started about 1700 by James Mitchell from Scalloway. The island was leased by Arthur Anderson, the founder of P&O, in 1837, when he set up the Shetland Fishery Company, which was designed to break the *"truck"* system whereby the "landowners" controlled the fishing by owning the boats and equipment as well as the catches. In 1893 Herbert Anderton, a rich Yorkshireman, bought the island, and extended the *Haa'* to make Vaila Hall the largest house in Shetland.

Papa Stour and Sandness aerial from south east

The road to **SANDNESS** crosses loch-studded moorland, which gives way to the fertile township. There are "Norse" mills and a broch at Huxter, a Burnt Mound at Crawton and a promontory fort at Ness of Garth as well as a modern wool spinning mill. There are also several chambered cairns, notably the Spinner (HU216562) and Gallow Hill (HU257507) - ruinous but interesting.

WEST BURRAFIRTH (ON *Borgarfjoror* - Broch Firth) is another remote harbour, and is the departure point for the ferry to Papa Stour. Burnt Mounds, Brochs and Norse Mills are much in evidence again. Even more remote is the Voe of Snarraness, another good place to seek out Otters.

Culswick Broch interior

Scord of Brouster

Westerwick

Vaila

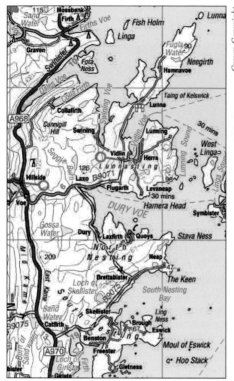

North Voe of Gletness

Laxo Voe

NESTING (ON *Nes Ting*) The *ting* was held at Ness of Neap, off which there is an Iron Age promontory fort (HU508580) on Hog Island. The many prehistoric houses, cairns, burnt mounds and at least two brochs attest to the early importance of this area for settlement.

The **Loch of Girlsta** is said to be named after Geirhilda, daughter of Hrafna Floki who was tragically drowned here in about 870 while they were on their way to Iceland, which island her father is said to have named. Arctic Char as well as Brown Trout live in this rather sombre loch.

Although the main road north is fast it runs through rather desolate country. In contrast, the winding roads which run through North and South Nesting are full of interest with many sheltered bays, small lochs and evidence of ancient occupation.

Catfirth was used for seaplane operations during WWI, as a satellite to Scapa Flow, but was never fully developed and little now remains to be seen. Its small size meant that it was only usable in certain wind conditions, which is why Sullom Voe was selected as a base in WWII.

Although most of Nesting is low-lying there is a steep hill at Kirk Ward and a very fine view from the top of nearby **Bow Field** (HU467577, 151m) where a watch tower was built in WWI. The low-lying coast here makes for excellent walking, and the **Moul of Eswick** with its lighthouse, or the **Hill of Neap** on Stava Ness make pleasant destinations. Seals, Puffins, Black Guillemots and Ravens as well as abundant wild flowers add to the scene.

The many small lochs and little streams make the area attractive to Otters, which frequent many of the shores, especially near outfalls of streams. The numerous tidal inlets, notably those at Catfirth, Vassa Voe, Vadill of Garth, Dury and Laxo are attractive to waders, while sea ducks and divers may be seen in the voes, especially in winter.

LUNNASTING (ON *Hlunn-eid*, from *hlunnr* - a roller to help beach boats) is separated from Nesting by Dury Voe, at whose head, Laxo has an ayre and salt flats which are very attractive to migrating waders which may be closely observed from the car. The ferry to Whalsay runs from here normally.

Laxo Voe - a good place for waders and sea ducks as well as Otters

The present St Margaret's, **Lunna Kirk**, was built in 1753 near the site of a much earlier chapel, and incorporates some of the ancient walls. Buttresses support the east wall which also has a peephole for lepers, so that they could hear the service without entering the church. The interior is original - the pulpit is surrounded on three sides by a gallery accessed from an outside stair.

Vidlin Voe from the south west

Lunna House dates from 1660 and was used as the first base for the *"Shetland Bus"*, before the operation moved to Scalloway in 1942. West Lunna Voe was the sheltered and remote anchorage. This clandestine operation forced the Germans to maintain a huge occupying force in Norway throughout the war, and despite early losses was regarded as being very successful. Lunnaness has exposures of ancient gneiss rock and there are Red-throated Divers on many of the small lochs.

Fish-drying beach at East Lunna Voe

St Margaret's Kirk with Lunna House in the background

Vidlin (ON *Vadill* - ford) is situated at the head of a very scenic voe with a sheltered harbour. The contrasting rock types with limestone on the east side and gneiss on the west show particularly clearly the difference in fertility of the soils.

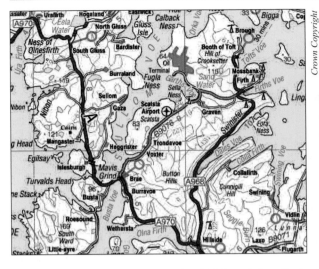

Crown Copyright

DELTING (ON *Dalr Ting* - Dale Ting) takes its name from the spectacular glacial U-shaped Dales Voe which is on the road to the ferry terminal for Yell at Toft. The island of Fora Ness (ON *Fornes* - promontory) is joined to the Mainland by an unusual treble ayre, enclosing The Houp (ON *Hopi* - Small Bay). Even if rushing for the ferry it is worthwhile stopping to take in the panoramic views from here.

VOE (ON *Vagr* - sheltered bay). lies at the head of Olna Firth and is a delightfully pretty spot. In the 1800s it developed as a Herring station and commercial centre. Today it has a small marina and retains a Scandinavian feel.

T.M. ADIE & SONS The story of T.M. Adie & Sons is an example of Shetland resourcefulness but also a warning about how to react

to change and globalisation. In 1830 Thomas Adie from Voe, aged 16, bought a sack of flour in Lerwick. He carried it home and sold it around the houses.

This was the start of a business that was to last until 1991. As a General Merchant the firm traded in local products, including fish and knitwear, which were often bartered for groceries and other essentials.

When the local fishery declined due to the advent of steam trawlers, the knitwear and weaving part of the business was greatly expanded. In the 1920s Shetland Tweed became a popular product and until the 1970s classic woolen garments were in high demand.

The advent of oil, with the resultant changes in the local economy, combined with globalisation resulted in the

The Busta standing stone, with Busta Voe and Brae in the background

Voe and Olna Firth from the east

demise of the company in 1991. The Shetland Museum retains a wide range of artefacts relating to the activities of the Company.

Perhaps its most famous product was the *"Everest"* jumpers, worn by Sir Edmund Hillary and Tensing Norgay on their 1953 ascent. The firm supplied Shetland knitwear to many polar and mountain expeditions over the years.

BRAE (ON *Breid-eid* - Broad Isthmus) sprawls along the north of Busta Voe and owes its development to the nearby Sullom Voe Oil Terminal. It offers many convenient facilities including a large leisure centre with a swimming pool and a supermarket.

Across the voe, **Busta House**, now a hotel, was once the seat of the Gifford family, who were descended from a Scottish minister who developed a taste for land which he acquired by most-

ly dubious means. The dynasty came to an end when the four sons were drowned while rowing across the Voe. It is not recorded whether or not they were sober. Family arguments over the succession lasted for years and finally bankrupted the estate.

TOFT (ON *Topt* - House site) is the ferry terminal for the North Isles. In the early morning or late evening this

can be a good place to catch sight of an Otter, while Yell Sound is one of the best places to see cetaceans such as Porpoises, Dolphins or Killer Whales in Shetland.

The road north from Voe has several interesting viewpoints, including the long Dales Voe and the double tombolo at Fora Ness. From Tofts there is a fine panorama of Yell Sound.

Tensing and Hillary on Mount Everest in 1953

Royal Geographic Society

The Hams O'Muckle Roe are especially pretty at sunset - North Ham

MUCKLE ROE (ON, *Raudey Mikla* - Big Red Isle) is composed of red granite rock, which resists erosion, and has resulted in spectacular coastal scenery, especially on the west side.

The island is joined to the Mainland by a bridge (another good Otter hunting spot), and apart from crofts on the east side is mostly moorland, with many small lochs. There are charming views up Busta Voe and over Swarbacks Minn from the road. The walking is rough but the thin vegetation at least means dry feet.

The **Hams O'Muckle Roe** (HU302660) are one of Shetland's best kept secrets. They can be reached by a walk along a track from **Little Ayre** (HU322628), and are best visited on a summer's evening, when the setting sun intensifies the redness of the rock.

The abandoned settlement of Ham has an interesting ruined watermill, but must have been very remote. **Erne Stack** (HU305671), once a breeding place for the Sea Eagle, is now home to a small Cormorant colony as is **Grusterwick** (HU296648). If time permits a return via Stromness, the most westerly point, and the south coast, passing several small stacks and geos makes an interesting walk. Perhaps the best views of the island are from seaward, especially on a summer's evening when returning from a fishing trip.

Bridge across Roe Sound

Ruined croft at Sandhill, Muckle Roe

SWARBACKS MINN was used in WWI as the anchorage for the 10th Cruiser Squadron, which consisted of British passenger liners which had been requisitioned by the Admiralty. These big ships were largely unsuited for a role as warships due to their vulnerability and fuel consumption.

The 10th Cruiser Squadron was used to blockade the North Sea from Norway to well into the Northern Approaches. 41 different passenger ships were armed with guns up to 6-inch calibre, so relieving a large number of Royal Navy vessels for other duties. During the war 17 were sunk, mainly by U-boats, although the *Oceanic* was lost off Foula due to navigational incompetence.

Swarbacks Minn on a placid evening

Vementry and Swarbacks Minn evening light

Cormorant (Scarf) on the nest

Ruined croft at Sandhill, Muckle Roe

Sullom Voe and the Oil Terminal from Sullom

SULLOM VOE (ON *Solheimarvagr* - Sunnyhome Voe) is an extension of Yell Sound, and its sheltered waters were tranquil until 1939, when the RAF established a flying boat base here. *SS Manela* was the base ship until shore facilities were built.

The first German bomb to land on British soil exploded at Sullom on 13 November 1939, killing a rabbit, and ensuring the popularity of the song *"Run Rabbit Run"*.

AA cruiser *HMS Coventry* was moored here for air defence, but German attacks soon showed that fighter defence was needed.

Sumburgh was unsuitable for *Spitfires*, but *Gladiators* were based there until **RAF Scatsta** was built after a massive operation where about 400,000m³ of peat was removed. Shoreside facilities were developed at Graven, and by war's end there was a considerable sprawling base here, which was soon to be abandoned.

The main activity of the base was anti-submarine and convoy escort patrols. *Catalinas* and *Sunderlands* were the main aircraft types based here, and had considerable success in attacking and sinking U-boats. Although some aircraft were lost due to enemy action, many more were written off by accidents and breakdowns.

The airfield at **Scatsta** saw limited use in WWII, with occasional detachments of *Spitfires*, and was also used as an emergency landing site by *Mosquitos* and *Lancasters* involved in attacks on Norway, especially during operations against *Tirpitz*.

Scatsta airfield was to lie derelict until 1978, when it was refurbished and used for oil-related flights during the construction of the **Oil Terminal**. The airfield continues to be used by many aircraft, both fixed wing and helicopters, involved in the oil industry.

German Luftwaffe reconnaissance image from 1940

Shetland Museum

In the early 1970s oil was discovered under the North Sea, and Sullom Voe was chosen as the most suitable location for tankers to load petroleum carried ashore by pipelines. Over 6,000 workers were employed in the construction phase, during which huge amounts of peat were again moved.

BP operates the terminal, which covers about 400ha, and handles oil from the Brent and Ninian pipeline systems which carry petroleum from the oilfields east of Shetland. Its throughput peaked in 1984 at over 58 million tonnes, but this has fallen to nearer 30 million tonnes today. Oil money has had a big effect on the Shetland economy, and the terminal looks set to operate for a long time to come.

Sullom Voe remains an excellent place for wildlife enthusiasts, with Otters quite common. The contrasts between the old crofts, wartime remains, oil industry facilities and the tranquil landscape are strong, and yet the Oil Terminal manages to blend with its surroundings remarkably well.

The **Houb of Scatsta** (HU397730) to the east of the airfield is one of the best places in Shetland to observe waders, especially during migration times. The whole Sullom Voe area is home to large numbers of wintering Eider, Long-tailed Duck, Grebes, Velvet Scoter and Great Northern Diver. Rarities such as White-billed Diver or King Eider show up quite often.

Scatsta airfield is again busy, now with oil-related traffic

Sullom Voe Oil Terminal today - it blends into the landscape

Sunderland taking off

Catalina over Shetland

Shetland Museum

Shetland Museum

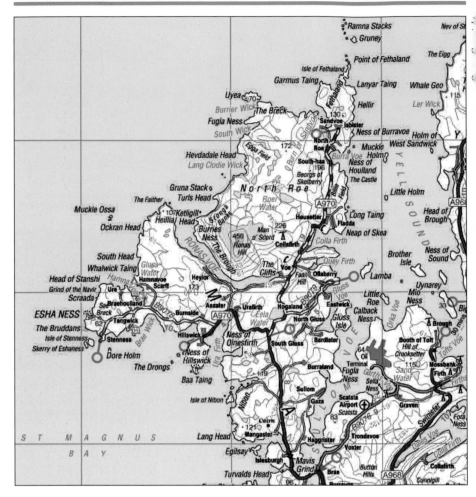

NORTHMAVINE (ON *Nordan Maefeidinn* - North of *Maef-eid*, the narrow isthmus) is joined to the rest of the mainland by **Mavis Grind**, a narrow isthmus which was formerly used to portage boats from the North Sea to the Atlantic. This very diverse peninsula has some of Shetland's best scenery including the cliffs at **Eshaness**, the highest hill, **Ronas Hill** and the wild country of **North Roe**. It has something for everyone regardless of season or weather.

The geology of this area is quite complex, with exposures of Lewissian gneiss in the Uyea area. Most of the east side is schist and gneiss, while Ronas Hill and the west is pink granite and Eshaness is composed of volcanic rocks and Old Red Sandstone. Small outcrops of limestone, as at Ollaberry, also occur, and give rise to much

Mavis Grind (ON Maef-eid Grind - Gate of the Narrow Isthmus)

more fertile soils than elsewhere.

Just north of Mavis Grind is **Islesburgh** chambered cairn (HU693685), a fine example of a *heel-shaped* cairn in a lovely location overlooking Minn. At nearby **Punds Water** (HU325713) another chambered cairn and prehistoric house are both well preserved.

Side roads such as those leading to Sullom in the east or Gunnister and Nibon in the west are well worth exploring for their lovely views. The body of *"Gunnister Man"* was found in a peat bank overlooking Glussdale Water in 1951. He was dressed in fine woollen garments and died, perhaps of exposure, in the 1600s. The elusive Otter is present in much of the area, and many of the lochs have Red-throated Divers.

At Urafirth a broad shingle bar enclosing a salt marsh is a good place to find the Oyster Plant. This is one of the largest of many such areas at the heads of voes which are attractive to waders. Sullom Voe is a major wintering area for divers and sea duck.

In the settlement of **Hillswick** (ON *Hidisvik* - Hlidi's Bay), a fine wooden hotel, the St Magnus Bay Hotel, originally built by the shipping company, makes a fine base or place for a meal. The nearby **Drongs** (HU260755) and the Isle of Westerhouse are a remarkable set of stacks off the **Ness of Hillswick**, whose west coast is particularly dramatic. It is well worth the short walk, either on a fine evening or even better when a high sea is running.

Shetland Museum

Punds Water chambered cairn

Mangaster Voe with Egilsay, Walls, Foula and Papa Stour in the background

The small lighthouse on Baa Taing was built to aid the navigation of the steamers which ran to Hillswick with cargo and passengers, many of whom were coming to stay in the hotel.

Otters really do cross here!

Hillswick from the south east

Sandwick on the road to Eshaness, with the Ness of Hillswick

ESHANESS (ON *Esjanes - esja* refers to the easily split, ashy volcanic rock) has jagged cliffs of Old Red Sandstone with volcanic basalt, andesite, lava and ignumbrite which have spectacular stacks, geos and blow holes.

Near the lighthouse, which was built by the Stevensons in 1921, **Calder's Geo** is very impressive. To the north a series of geos, stacks and caves each vie with each other, but perhaps the **Grind O'da Navir** is the most dramatic. Whether on a fine summer's day, in thick fog, during a big storm, or at sunset, Eshaness is always different.

The **Broch of Houlland** (HU215790) is unusual in that it is built on a small island on a loch without a good seaward view. At **Burnside** (HU281784) on the way to Eshaness is a crescent-shaped burnt mound with an intact cooking trough. The remains of **Cross Kirk**, an ancient chapel destroyed by a minister who felt it infringed his religion has interesting gravestones.

At **Stenness** the ruins of a *Haaf* fishing station, sheltered by the Isle of Stenness recall the dangerous work of offshore fishing with small open *sixareens*.

Rough seas at Eshaness

Dore Holm lies south of Utstabi (ON *Yztrboer* - Outermost Farm) and has variously been compared with an elephant or a dinosaur. That its natural arch should survive winter storms seems impossible.

Tangwick *Haa'* Museum illustrates Northmavine life over the years. It was built in the 17th century by the Cheynes, a Scottish family that "acquired" large estates in Shetland.

Johnny *"Notions"* Williamson of Hamnavoe invented his own vaccination cure for smallpox in the 18th century and saved many Shetlanders from this dangerous disease which formerly had claimed a lot of lives. His cottage has been renovated and turned into a "camping bod".

To the north of Eshaness the attractive little settlement of **Hamnavoe**, with its sheltered bay, ruined broch and standing stones is the starting point for a spectacular coastal walk along the **Villans O'Hamnavoe**. The sheer power of the Atlantic can be seen here on a stormy day. Huge blocks of rock have been flung inland by the waves, which have carved fantastic

Dore Holm - ON Dyrraholmr - Door Holm - has a large natural arch

shapes out of the cliffs.

From the top of the hill at the north end (HU254855, 107m) there are very good views over Ronas Hill and the Lang Ayre, as well as down Ronas Voe.

Inland the many small lochs are home to many Red-throated Divers, while Whimbrel and Golden Plover also nest here. Although only a few seabirds nest on the cliffs here, Eshaness is a good place for seawatching during bird migration times, and is also one of the best places to see whales or dolphins.

Tangwick Haa'Museum

Eshaness lighthouse

Ronas Voe from Heylor, where a Dutch frigate was surprised by the Royal Navy in 1674

RONAS (ON *Raudnes* - Red Ness from *raudr*, red) is the most remote and only mountainous part of the Mainland. The red granite has eroded to form beautiful cliffs at Ronas Voe and above the magnificent sweep of **Lang Ayre,** one of Shetland's loveliest, yet least accessible beaches.

Ronas Voe was the site of a battle in 1674 between the Dutch frigate *Wapen van Rotterdam,*

which had chosen to shelter in the voe, and the Royal Navy frigate *Newcastle,* which had arrived to check out the Dutch vessel. The Brits won the day, and an unknown number of Dutchmen were buried at **Hollanders' Knowe** (HU302807).

In April 1867, after being ice-bound off Greenland for 6 months, the Hull whaler *Diana* arrived at Ronas Voe. 13 of the ship's crew of 50 had died on the

14-month trip, including the captain. There is a memorial to those lost on Victoria Pier in Lerwick. A Norwegian whaling station operated from here in the early 20th century, but fortunately its lethal activites did not last long.

On **Ronas Hill** itself (HU315845, 450m) with its blockfields, wind and frost features and alpine plants there is much to interest the nature lover. Views from the top on a clear day encompass all of Shetland, but unfortunately the hill often wears a mantle of mist.

The summit is easily reached by driving to the top of **Collafirth Hill** (HU335835, 230m), where there is a derelict military installation. It is worth the drive just for the view. At the top is a well-preserved chambered cairn, with probably modern additions, but the only one in Shetland to have an intact roof. It provides a useful shelter from the blast for walkers to enjoy their picnics.

The steep 200m cliffs on the west coast are especially impressive. The shingle beaches of **Lang Ayre** and **Valla Kames** are hard to access but well worth the

View north towards Uyea from Ronas Hill

Stripes of rock debris on the side of Ronas Hill

effort. Grey Seals come ashore to have their pups in autumn along this coast. Inland northwards the area is studded with small lochs which support a large population of Red-throated Divers. Many waders and skuas also breed here. Relict trees and shrubs survive on small holms and other inaccessible places.

East of Ronas Hill there are several crofting communities, including **Ollaberry** with its fertile limestone. The township is also famous for its exposure of the **Walls Boundary Fault**, said to be the best example of a *"major tear fault"* in UK.

Below the **Beorgs of Housetter** (HU362855) what look like standing stones, the *"Giant's Stones"*, are in fact all that remains of what must have been

a very impressive chambered cairn. Nearby the chamber plan of another ruined cairn can be made out. A much better-preserved miniature chambered cairn (HU360855) is a challenge to find but has a fine view.

Further north the headland of **Fethaland** (ON *Feitiland* - Fatland) is an easy walk from Isbister (HU371910). Fethaland was the site of a major *Haaf* fishing station in the 19th century, when up to 60 *sixareens* worked from here. Outcrops of serpentine make the vegetation especially rich, and in summer the wild flowers here are wonderful, and include the Purple Saxifrage.

Off the Point of Fethaland, the **Ramna Stacks** (HU375975) are an RSPB reserve, and one of the few Shetland breeding grounds of Leach's Petrel. The headland

is also a very good place for sea-watching, whether for birds or whales.

On the east side at the **Kame of Isbister** (HU382915), which is a rocky headland accessible only by a very steep path, there are remains of a number of buildings, thought to be an early Christian monastic site. Interestingly, there is a similar site across Yell Sound at **Birrier of West Sandwick** (HU436916).

Uyea (HU319926) is joined to the Mainland by a lovely sandy ayre. The rocks here are Lewissian gneiss, some of the most ancient in the world. On the long walk in, the track passes the **Beorgs of Uyea** where the felsite used to make *"Shetland Knives"* is found (HU327900).

Fethaland - a beautiful headland with the remains of a haaf fishing station

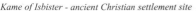

Kame of Isbister - ancient Christian settlement site

Point of Fethaland and the Ramna Stacks

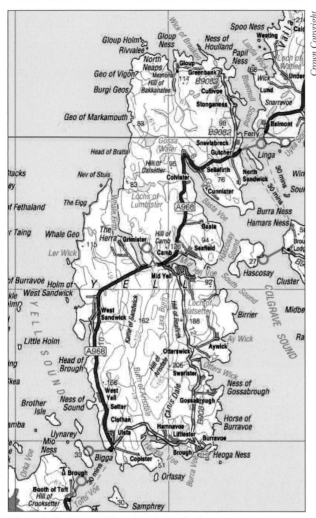

YELL (ON *Jala* - but probably pre-Norse and thus the derivation is obscure) is the largest of the North Isles and is reached by a 20-minute ferry trip across Yell Sound. Cetaceans such as Killer Whales, dolphins and porpoises are regularly seen here, as well as birds such as Gannets, divers, Guillemots and sea ducks.

Many people drive right across Yell on the way to Unst and get the impression that this island, 17 miles long and up to 7 miles across is nothing but a huge peat bog. It certainly has a lot of peat, perhaps 200 million tonnes of it, but it also has much for the visitor, especially its varied coastline with fine cliffs, sandy bays and many voes.

On the road north from Ulsta, the **Ness of Sound** is joined to Yell by a double shingle ayre, and very much merits a walk. Further north **West Sandwick** has a lovely sandy beach, backed by dunes and machair. Its sheltered harbour of **Southladie Voe** must have made this little area attractive to settlers from an early time.

Ulsta - the ferry terminal for Toft on the Mainland

North along the low cliffs, Birrier of West Sandwick is an early Christian monastic site with remains of about 13 buildings on a sloping stack joined to the land by a dangerous path which is not recommended.

At **Whalefirth** Yell is nearly split in two as Mid Yell Voe is only a mile away in the east. Whalefirth was famously used by German U-boats in WWI to lie up and also find some fine

"White Wife" of Queyon

Sunset down Yell Sound from Ness of Sound

fresh sheep to augment their diet. The supposedly haunted house of Windhoose is just by. The name does not mean "house", but ON *Vindass* - Windy Ridge. There is a ruined broch and a chambered cairn nearby.

Mid Yell with its school, leisure centre and shops is the main settlement of the island. From here a single-track road leads south past Aywick, Otterswick and Gossabrough to Burravoe. The Horse of Burravoe (HU535812) is a good place to see breeding seabirds, including Puffins, up close. Burravoe itself has an attractive little harbour, which was difficult for sailing vessels. The **Old *Haa'* of Burravoe** is now a museum, and was built about 1672, while the nearby ornate St Colman's Episcopal Church dates from 1900. The broch mound after which the village is named, has a *skeo*, a drystone building with holes in the walls used for drying fish or reestit mutton.

The ***"White Wife"* of Queyon**, on the north shore of Otterswick, is the figurehead of

the German cadet ship, *Bohus"* wrecked here in 1924 with the loss of three young men, who are buried at Mid Yell. The prominent memorial faces the sea .

Further north is the large inlet of

Old Haa' of Burravoe

Ness of Sound is attached to Yell by a double shingle ayre or tombolo

West Sandwick has a fine sandy beach and some remaining dunes

The Wick of Breakon is one of the loveliest beaches in Shetland

Basta Voe, once a favourite place to beach *Caa'in* Whales and now home to fish farms. Over the hill the ferry terminal to Unst and Fetlar at Gutcher is a pretty spot.

The small road along the north side of Basta Voe leads to Kirkabister, with its rather austere pony stud, a square Victorian structure used in the production of ponies in the 19th century for use in coal mines. At the east of **Burra Ness** (HU558957) the substantial remains of a lichen-covered broch guard the approaches.

An alternative scenic route is to take the small track from the head of Basta Voe at Dalsetter to Cullivoe. This passes prime birding country, and using the car as a hide Red-throated Diver, Dunlin, Whimbrel, Golden Plover and other species can be observed without disturbance.

West from Cullivoe with its new fishing pier **Gloup Voe** has a sad story to tell. In July 1881, 58 men were drowned whilst engaged in the *Haaf* fishing. A fierce storm blew up and 6 boats from here were lost. The poignant memorial commemorates those lost.

A coastal walk from here leads to the Iron Age promontory fort at **Burgi Geos** (HP473034). On the land side a series of upright stones led to a narrow path towards the fort. There are remains of field walls and clearance cairns nearby indicating prehistoric settlement.

The **Wick of Breakon** is one of

Broch at Burra Ness

Gloup memorial

the nicest beaches in the north of Shetland. The dunes and machair behind it have a quite different flora from most of Yell. The shifting sands cover a complex of remains of human settlement. Burials, pottery and ruins are present.

The **Kirk of Ness** (HP532049) has been largely overwhelmed by sand but is one of a very few remaining medieval churches in Shetland. It was abandoned in 1750. The nearby **Kirk Loch** is a haven for wildfowl and waders, especially during migration times. A ruined broch on Migga Ness, and possible Viking houses and a boat burial complete a fascinating place.

Yell is famous for its **Otters**, and though elusive they can with care be closely observed here. They feed in the sea on small fish, which they catch along shallow shores. However they are not truly marine and need a source of fresh water. Thus they are often to be seen near small water courses leading to the sea. Early morning or late evening are the best times. Otters have a very good sense of smell and hear well so stay downwind, and keep quiet.

The attractive island of **Hascosay** (ON *Hafskigsey* - sea wood or wood from the ocean) lies off Mid Yell and is a haven for birds and seals. Its position in **Colgrave Sound** (ON *kolgref* - charcoal burning pit) no doubt reflects the driftwood which used to collect here.

Red-throated Diver and chick - Rain Gjus

An Otter in the ebb - Draatsi

Laurie Campbell

Croft in East Yell

Regatta at Mid Yell

135

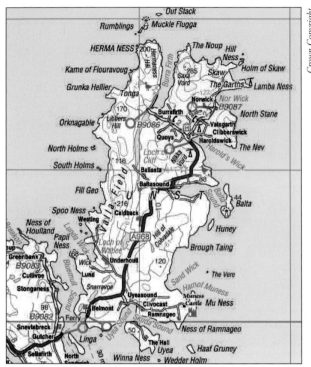

UNST (ON *Aumstr* - but probably pre-Norse and of obscure meaning) is reached by a short ferry ride from Gutcher in Yell. **Blue Mull Sound** is a regular flight path for Gannets and Guillemots. In winter Eider and Black Guillemot are often seen in large flocks, while cetaceans like Killer Whales are also seen.

In contrast to Yell, the geology of Unst is complex and unusual. The westside from Belmont to Saxavord is composed of ancient gneiss and schist in various blocks. A wide band of serpentine runs up the centre of the island, while the south east is greenstone. There are outcrops of steatite in the north and a rough granite at Skaw. The varied geology has led to a wide variety of habitats, which include blanket bog, extensive cliffs, sandy beaches with machair systems, fertile marshy meadows and grassland, serpentine debris fields, herb-rich heaths and fertile limestone areas.

Before heading up the island it is worth taking a stroll to **Hoga Ness** (HP558005) with its ruined **Belmont Broch** and well-preserved twin ramparts. There are fine views over Blue Mull Sound from here. The decaying finery of nearby 18th century Belmont House is in stark contrast to the nearby abandoned crofts at Snarravoe.

The pretty settlement of **Uyeasound** is sheltered by Uyea (ON *Eyju* - to the island). At the pier the roofless stone shell of Greenwell's Booth, built about 1700 for local traders, the Scotts, is a reminder that this was once a busy fishing station. The **Galley Shed** is home to Uyeasound Up Helly Aa galley and makes an interesting visit. **Easter Loch** is a good place to

Muness Castle was built about 1598 and burnt down in 1627

Muness Castle entrance

observe wintering wildfowl from the car.

There are two standing stones at **Clivocast** which are prominent in this bare landscape. The one nearer the road (HP60607) is about 3m high but quite slim.

Muness Castle was built about 1598 for the reviled Lawrence Bruce, bastard half-brother of Robert Stewart. It has variously been described as *"exquisite"* or *"like something out of a horror movie"*. Visitors must make up their own minds. Bruce is said to have left his Perthshire estate after killing someone in a brawl. He was appointed *Foud* of Shetland)deputy to Lord Robert Stewart in 1571), and he soon showed his family traits.

As *Foud* Bruce was in charge of collecting tax - *skat* - for the Earl and rapidly devised ways of cheating udallers out of their land and of altering the system of weights and measures to his own advantage. Despite the *"Complaint of the People of Orkney and Shetland"* in 1575 and subsequent investigation proving him guilty this rogue

Sandwick, site of Norse houses, a Pictish burial and an ancient chapel

was allowed to continue blithely on. His castle, paid for and built by Shetland *udallers*, did not last long as it was burnt down about 1627, variously by French privateers or as a result of a family feud.

In the sand dunes about half way along the beach at **Sandwick** (HP618023) is a ruined Norse farm dating from about 1300AD. It has a rectangular house and byre, enclosed in a yard. Perhaps of most note was the door to the byre which was wider at the top than the bottom to let cows through. Nearby a Pictish period burial cairn, the only one of its type so far found in Shetland, was carefully lined with upright flat stones and quartz pebbles.

The ruins of an ancient small chapel at **Framgord** (HP619029) on the north side of the bay are surrounded by a kirk-yard which has some very old small cross-slabs. There are also a number of coped headstones which are similar to hogback stones, but are straight-edged. They may be 12th or 13th century.

Cross-incised stone at Framgord

Clivocast standing stone

Easter Loch, Uyeasound

St Olaf's Kirk at Lunda Wick dates from the 12th century

WESTING has a variety of sites of interest and is reached by taking the first left after leaving Uyeasound. It owes its lushness to an outcrop of limestone. The importance of Blue Mull Sound in the Iron Age is clear from the number of brochs which line it - at least four on the Unst side and two on the Yell side.

There is a small, isolated broch at **Snabrough** (HP568028) with no seaward view, overlooking the **Loch of Snarravoe** which is a good site for wildfowl in winter. The much more impressive broch at **Underhoull** (HP574045) is situated on top of a steep rise. It is protected on the north side by two large earth ramparts with deep ditches. There is a superb view of Bluemull Sound and Lunda Wick from here.

Further on there is another broch situated on the rocky island of **Brough Holm**. Evidence of settlement is scattered all over the Westing area, including ruined crofts, field walls and prehistoric house sites.

One of the few visible **Norse farmsteads** in Shetland lies below the broch at Underhoull (HP574044). This complex of houses and outbuildings was excavated in the 1960s and has since been sadly neglected. An Iron Age house lies underneath the Norse structures. Although overgrown the outline and interior plans can be clearly made out. A large assembly of steatite artefacts was discovered here.

On the road to Lund, the standing stone of **Bordastubble** (HP578034) is the largest in Shetland, at over 3.5m high. It is probably of glacial origin. **Lunda Wick** is a very attractive bay, surrounded by fertile meadows. On the south side the 12th century **St Olaf's Kirk** is one of the few remaining Norse churches in Shetland.

Although the east gable is a later repair most of the rest of the building is intact. It was used until 1785. Original features include inclined door jambs with circular arches, small windows and the excellent stonework which has ensured its survival.

The kirkyard has a number of interesting cross-shaped grave markers, as well as headstones to two German merchants from Bremen who died in 1573 and 1585. On the former it says that *"Segebad Dekten had traded in this country for 52 years"*. One is inside the church. The inscriptions are now barely legible.

North on the main road the lochs should be checked for Red-throated Divers, other waterfowl and waders. There is a ruined chambered cairn near the road at **Loch of Watlee** (HP596051) and another on the top of the **Hill of Caldback** (HP608067), from which there is a wonderful panoramic view of the whole of Unst.

Norse farmstead at Underhoull, Westing, above Lunda Wick

Kirkaby and Brough Holm, Westing with North Yell in the background

Broch with impressive ramparts at Underhoull, Westing, above Lunda Wick

Bordastubble standing stone

Humorous tableau in a bus shelter

Lunda Wick is a beautiful sandy bay backed by green pasture

The remote and wild Woodwick and the steep Dale of Woodwick

BALTASOUND (ON *Balt-ey - Balti's Isle*) is one of the best natural harbours in Shetland, its entrance being sheltered by Balta, with its broch and small lighthouse. The harbour was very busy during the season in the Herring Boom of the late 19th and early 20th centuries.

The population multiplied severalfold, when hundreds of first sail-powered *Zulus* and later steam drifters filled the Sound to discharge their catches. Several thousand girls worked as gutters and packers, while coopers assembled barrels in which the Herring were preserved in salt for export mostly to Eastern Europe and Russia.

Unst's unusual geology has resulted in the availability of several minerals in commercially viable amounts. Chromite and Talc were produced in large quantities but the quarries have now closed. The Chromite was ground up at the **Hagdale Horse Mill** (HP541101).

Baltasound has the **most northerly Post Office** in the UK, where visitors can have their mail so stamped. Nearby, outside **Buness House** in 1817, the French physicist, Jean Biot, determined the strength of gravity with great precision as part of a study of the shape of the earth. Apparently the main reason for the studies was ballistics as the

French at the time thought their guns to be less accurate than the British ones.

Other interesting visitors have included the physicist Kator, also doing gravitational experiments, Lucien Bonaparte (Napoleon's nephew) researching Old Norse, Lady Franklin in search of her lost husband and his expedition and even grave robbers Burke and Hare who posed as clock menders.

Thomas Edmondston, who discovered the eponymous chickweed was accidentally killed in Peru at the age of 20 whilst on a scientific expedition which was to have met up with Franklin in Alaska. Buness House has a fascinating collection of artefacts and old books which visitors can peruse.

The Baltasound and Haroldswick areas are remarkably green and fertile compared to much of the island and support several herds of cattle, which is now unusual in Shetland. The marshy area and meadows between Haroldswick and Norwick is said to have the greatest variety of breeding birds in Shetland, as well as a very diverse flora.

On top of **Muckle Heog** (HP631108, 120m) are a large ruined chambered cairn and nearby, a smaller *heel-shaped* one. The enigmatic **Rounds of Tivla** are near the south side of the summit of **Crussa Field** (HP616107, 130m). Only one now survives of what may be Bronze Age burial enclosures.

Skaw beach is the most northerly in the UK

A central stony area is surrounded by three low, concentric banks, separated by shallow ditches.

Haroldswick is said to be named after King Harald Fairhair who moored his fleet here about 875AD when he was bringing the Shetland Vikings under control. Not content with just raiding Britain and Ireland they had taken to raiding Norway too - not quite the thing to do.

At Haroldswick the **Unst Boat Haven** has several preserved traditional wooden boats and a large number of interesting artefacts and displays about the sea and fishing. The nearby **Unst Heritage Centre** has displays on geology, history, genealogy and, of course, knitting and spinning.

Talc is still quarried at Klibberswick, above which lie the remains of **Cross Kirk** (HP650121), where women used to pray for the safety of their men at sea.

Norwick is an especially attractive little bay, backed by a marshy area which is very colourful with wild flowers in summer, and also an excellent place for birds, as has been mentioned. Within the interesting graveyard there are some ancient grave markers and the foundations of **St John's Chapel.** Recent excavations have uncovered what may be an early Norse grave.

Further on is the most northerly inhabited house in the UK, at

Unst Boat Haven, Haroldswick

Baltasound was very busy during the Herring Boom

Shetland Museum

Skaw, with a fine beach below it. Lamba Ness has the remains of the northern end of Britain's WWII radar system, still waiting to be cleared up after 65 years. Its modern equivalent sits atop Saxavord.

St John's Church at Baliasta (HP602095) dates from 1764, but it stands on the site of a much older church which would have been demolished at the time. There are some interesting gravestones in the kirkyard and within the shell of the kirk.

The remote Dale of Woodwick and **Woodwick** itself can be reached via **Houllna Gruna** (HP590113, 140m) from which there are fine views over Loch of Cliff to Burra Firth and Saxavord.

Puffins at Hermaness

Edmondston's Mouse-ear Chickweed (Cerastium nigrescens) is unique to Unst and flowers from June to August

KEEN OF HAMAR (ON *Hamar* - rocky outcrop on a hillside, *keen* may mean bright and may be pre-Norse) is a large serpentenite debris field, and is host to a fascinating range of plants. Much of the area has little vegetation and the action of the weather continues to break the rock into smaller and smaller pieces. However, in places small accumulations of sandy soil allow patches of vegetation to flourish.

Edmondston's Chickweed, first recorded by Thomas Edmondston in 1837, is unique to the area, but plants such as Hoary Willow Grass, Northern Rock Cress, Norwegian Sandwort, St John's Wort, Kidney Vetch and Moss Campion also grow here. Several salt-adapted species such as Scurvy Grass, Thrift and Sea Plantain also thrive.

Suggested reasons for the poor vegetation cover range from the presence of heavy metals such as chromium to a lack of nutri-ents, but it is now thought that the serpentinite debris drains the water so well that it behaves like a *"wet desert"*. Many of the plants which thrive here do in fact have adaptations such as thick leaves, hairy exposed surfaces and deep roots.

On the north of the hill stripes can be seen where stones of different sizes have become sorted by the action of freezing and thawing. Normally this only occurs on mountain tops, but here it is observed at 50m.

Serpentinite debris field, Keen of Hamar

Northern Rock Cress

The Gord, Hermaness and Muckle Flugga from Saxavord

HERMANESS (ON *Hermunurnes* - Hermunr's Ness) is home to one of the largest seabird breeding colonies in Britain. The stacks, ledges and banks of the coastline and the blanket bog of the interior support at least 100,000 breeding pairs including 12,000 Gannet, 25,000 Puffin, 14,000 Fulmar, 20,000 Guillemot, 1,000 Razorbill, 1,000 Kittiwake, 800 Bonxie, 400 Shag as well as Arctic Skua, Black Guillemot and Gulls.

There is a Scottish Natural Heritage **Visitor Centre** in the old lighthouse shore station at **Burrafirth** (HP613149), which should be visited before following the path around the headland, which takes about 4 hours. There used to be a hut about halfway, but it was blown away in a fierce storm, sadly with the loss of the Canadian couple sheltering there.

The cliffs and stacks from Saito to the Taing of Looswick hold most of the breeding birds, with Gannets crowding the stacks and Guillemots the ledges, while Puffins breed in burrows on the grassy banks and may be approached quite closely. Bonxies nest in the heathland and are very aggressive at defending their eggs and young. Although they will dive-bomb people, they rarely actually hit anyone, unlike Terns, which may well draw blood.

MUCKLE FLUGGA (ON *Mikla Flugey* - large precipice island) and Outstack (ON *Utstak* - Outer Stack) at 60°51'N, 0°53'W are the most northerly islands in Britain. The lighthouse was built in 1858 during the Crimean War by David and Thomas Stevenson, unusually of brick, due to the exposed and difficult location. In large storms seas can break right over the 66m high light which has been automatic since 1995.

Muckle Flugga lighthouse with visitors

Buness House

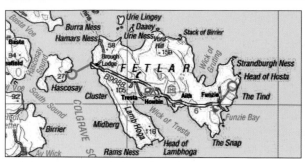

Snowy Owl

FETLAR (ON *Fetill* - band or strap, perhaps referring to the *Funzie Girt*, an ancient dyke which divides the island) was always described as Wast Isle and East Isle and has been described as the *"Garden of Shetland"* on account of its fertile soils. The geology is mostly serpentinite, here supporting a flora of grassland rich in wild flowers. The headland of Lamb Hoga in the south east is gneiss, while the east coast near Funzie is conglomerate.

Apart from the dyke there is further evidence of human occupation. The enigmatic **Hjaltadans** (HU618928) where a ring of large stones surrounds a shallow ditch, with two larger stones at the centre may date from the Bronze Age. The centre stones are said to be a fiddler and his wife who were surprised by the dawn which turned the surrounding dancing trows and the couple to stone as the sun rose.

The importance of Fetlar in Iron Age times is clear from the number of brochs. Two guard the Wick of Tresta at **Houbie** (HU620903) and **Aith** (HU629901). Another two overlook Colgrave Sound and Yell, which has a similar row of brochs. There is a small fort at **Aithbank** (HU629901) with three ramparts. What may be a Viking boat burial lies above the west shore of the Wick of Aith.

Overlooking the pier at Houbie the **Ripple Stone** is prominent but of unknown antiquity. Nearby the **Fetlar Interpretative Centre** has a wealth of information on the island as well as regularly changing exhibitions.

Ruins of what is thought to be a large Norse monastic site on Outer and Inner Brough at **Strandburgh Ness** ((HP670930) have not yet been investigated. There may be a link between the two in the past. The isolated stack of the Clett (HU642944) also has ruined buildings and may be related.

The island had a population of 761 in 1841 but the "owner" decided that sheep were better than people were and soon cleared most of the island, using crofthouse and broch stones to build his now-decaying folly at Brough. Sadly the population of this delightful island has never recovered.

Wick of Aith with Wick of Tresta and Lamb Hoga in background

Laurie Campbell

Red-necked Phalarope on Loch of Funzie   *Whimbrel - the airstrip is a good place to see them*

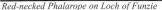

As elsewhere in Shetland the fishermen were bound to their landlords under the iniquitous *"truck"* system whereby the former were entirely dependent on the latter, and often little better than slaves.

Fetlar has a wealth of wildlife to view, especially breeding birds and wild flowers in summer. Most of the UK population of **Red-necked Phalarope** nest on the island and they may often be seen feeding on the Loch of Funzie or from the RSPB hide. Whimbrel, Arctic Skua, Arctic Tern, Bonxie, Golden Plover and Dunlin all favour the dry heathland, while many of the lochs hold Red-throated Diver.

Seabirds, including Manx Shearwater and a large colony of Storm Petrel breed along the cliffs of Lamb Hoga. Perhaps

View north from Stackaberg

Wick of Tresta and Lamb Hoga

Fetlar's greatest claim to fame was the Snowy Owl, which bred here from 1967 to 1975. Sadly none have been seen here since 1985.

Otters are common on Fetlar and perhaps the best place to look out for them is at the ferry terminal. Common and Grey Seals breed on the small islands off the north coast, especially

around Urie Ness.

Access to the **RSPB Reserve** is restricted from May to September, however all of the bird species mentioned can be seen from the roadside, or otherwise outwith the Reserve. The warden should be consulted about access to the Funzie Girt and Hjaltadans during the restricted period.

147

WHALSAY

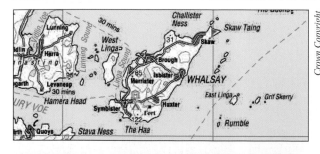

"Bremen Bod" is a restored 17th century trading "booth" at Symbister

WHALSAY (ON *Hvalsey - hvalr*, whale island) does not have the fertile soils of Fetlar, being composed of gneiss, and its inhabitants have always depended on the sea for a living. Despite this the island has gained the well deserved nickname *"The Bonny Isle."*

First impressions on stepping ashore here are of wonder with the fleet of modern fishing boats, large numbers of new and impressive houses and obvious prosperity. Whalsaymen took part in the *Haaf* fishing and in the Herring Boom, but it was only after WWII that development really started. The first large purse-seine vessel arrived in 1969 and since then the fleet has been continuously upgraded and expanded.

Today the large fleet of modern vessels, all owned by their crews, forms a large part of Shetland's fishing industry. Crofting, by contrast, plays a very small role in the economy of the island, with only a few sheep now being kept.

There is considerable evidence of early settlement on the island. On the eastern slope of **Gamla Vord** a whole series of prehistoric structures may be seen. The **Benie Hoose** (HU586653) and the nearby **Standing Stones of Yoxie** (HU587653) are similar to other prehistoric houses in Shetland. There are several possible chambered cairns in the vicinity.

Near the **Loch of Sandwick** (HU536618) several ancient houses and field walls can be made out. At Brough (HU555651) there are peck marks on a rock, which may date from the Bronze Age, while at the top of **Symbister Hill** (HU533620) there is a chambered cairn with a wonderful view.

On the **Loch of Huxter** (HU558620) a small holm is connected to the shore by a causeway. A blockhouse and wall protect the holm. Most of the stones have been used to build the nearby planticrubs. There is a large broch mound at Brough, on the west side.

Symbister (ON *Sunnbolstadr* - South Farm) has a perfect natural harbour, sheltered from the north by West Linga and home to the fishing fleet and pleasure craft. The **Bremen Bod** on the east side of the bay is a 17th century Hanseatic trading booth, which is now an interpretation centre.

One of Whalsay's large fishing vessels at Symbister

The **Old *Haa'*** across *"Bremen Strasse"* was the base of the Scottish Bruces until the last of them built Symbister House, an incongruous Georgian mansion which is now part of the school. It is said that this Bruce built the house so that his heirs would have no money.

The Yoxie House is a typical Shetland prehistoric homestead

The poet Christopher Grieve (a.k.a. **Hugh MacDiarmid**) lived at Sudheim (or Sodom on the map) from 1933 to 1942 and, despite poverty and illness, wrote some of his best works during this time. When I met him in the 1960s he certainly had good things to say about Whalsay. His former house is now a camping bod.

Although not famous for its wildlife, Whalsay is a good place to be in the bird migration time, with its easterly location and many gardens which may attract vagrants. Symbister Harbour, **The Houb at Kirkness** and all of the lochs are good places to seek out birds. Otters are often seen around Symbister, where they have become habituated to traffic in the harbour.

Traditional Shetland yoles are now frequently involved in rowing races

Wooden sculpture outside Symbister School

During late spring and summer much of Whalsay becomes a carpet of wild flowers due to the lack of heavy grazing by sheep. The walking is easy over most of the heathland. There is a small but fine sandy beach at Sandwick at the south end.

At Skaw at the north end is Shetland's most northerly golf course, while Symbister boasts a leisure centre with a swimming pool.

Symbister Leisure Centre

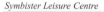

OUT SKERRIES

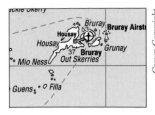

(OUT) SKERRIES (ON *Ut sker* - Out Skerries), Shetland's most easterly islands, consist of three small islands and a number of skerries. They are mostly composed of ancient gneiss but a band of crystalline limestone runs through the middle of the group, resulting in a fertile area around the perfect natural harbour of Bod Voe.

The main islands of **Bruray** (ON *Brurey* - Bridge Isle) and **Housay** (ON *Husey*, House Isle) have long been joined by a bridge. Locally they are known as East and West Isle. **Grunay** (ON *Groeney* - Green Isle) forms the south eastern side of the harbour and is separated from Housey by the Northeast and Sooth Mooths.

The lighthouse was built in 1858 on **Bound Skerry**. It was automated in 1972 but its accommodation and fine garden on Grunay now lie abandoned. In WWII German planes made several low level attacks, one of which killed a keeper's wife. Also in WWII a British *Beaufort* aircraft on its way back from a raid on Norway crash-landed on Grunay, sadly with the loss of the three crew.

There is very little evidence of ancient man here, except for the enigmatic **"Battle Pund"** (HU683714), a roughly rectangular setting of stones about 13m wide, which may be Bronze Age. There are also a number of small ruins, some of which may have been chambered cairns.

The ancient system of *"rigs"*, where the arable land was divided into strips which were cultivated in rotation, survived longer here than anywhere else. Despite virtually all of the udallers losing their land to the Scots "lairds", and the iniquitous *"truck"* system, the isolation, fertile land and nearby rich fishing grounds meant that the people were always able to keep enough for themselves.

Fishing has always been very important to the Skerries folk, and today several boats work from here. There is also a large communally-owned salmon farm. It is as though the sea is in their blood. The author recently observed two *"peerie boys"* working their small creel boat. Every action was as if inborn. This is of course why Shetlanders have for long been in such demand as seamen.

Being so far east, Skerries is one of the first landfalls for birds in the migration seasons. In misty weather all sorts of rarities can turn up here. The other airbourne visitor, the Loganair *Islander*, is the easiest way to get to the Skerries, but be warned - the runway is extremely short!

Vase from "Kennemerland"

Bod Voe with its Northeast and Sooth Mooths is sheltered by Grunay

There is a good view of Skerries from the lighthouse

Over the years many ships have been wrecked here. Perhaps the most famous are two Dutch East Indiamen *Kennemerland* which was wrecked in December 1664, with only three survivors and the *De Leifde*, from which there was only one survivor. In both cases much was salvaged at the time, but recent underwater archaeology has turned up a number of interesting artefacts, some of which may be seen at Lerwick Museum.

The enigmatic "Battle Pund" is on the slope to the west of the harbour

One severe problem for the Skerries folk is water supply. The small catchment area and largely impermeable rocks mean that frequently water has to be shipped in. An ingenious system has been installed to help catch more run-off, but in dry summers lack of water is still a problem.

The excellent harbour of Bod Voe

Water catchment drain

The lighthouse on Bound Skerry is built of brick and was first lit in 1858

PAPA STOUR

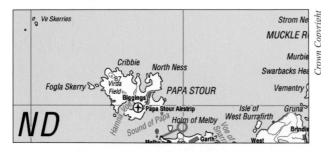

PAPA STOUR (ON *Papey Stora*, *Papi*, priest, *storr*, large - Large Isle of the Papar) has perhaps the best cliff scenery in Shetland or even the UK. The red cliffs are formed from volcanic rhyolite which have eroded into a fantastic series of stacks, caves, arches, geos and skerries. Basalt and Old Red Sandstones underlie the rhyolite which forms much of the island.

The views from the coast are spectacular enough, but in settled weather an exploration by boat is said to be quite exceptional, and many writers have waxed lyrical after such a trip. Perhaps the most spectacular is **Kirstan**

Hole (HU15365) where a cave has partially collapsed to form a gloup. The scenery is best either on a fine summer's evening, or during a fierce winter storm.

All of the habitations are on the more fertile east end of the island, while most of the west end has been *"scalped"* over the centuries to provide fuel, turves for roofs and to improve the croftland as well as bedding for animals. Nevertheless the thin remaining soil is fertile and supports a wide variety of plants such that on foggy summer days fishermen could find their way home by following the scent of the wild flowers.

Seabirds including Bonxie, Arctic Skua and sometimes large numbers of Arctic Tern breed here as well as waders and a few Red-throated Divers. It is not generally a good island for migrants.

Although there is evidence of ancient settlement there is not much to be seen in the way of archaeological remains, presumably because the stones were reused repeatedly. Several burnt mounds are scattered over the east end of the island.

Excavations at **Biggings** (ON *Bygd* - Village) uncovered remains of a structure with wooden walls and floor dating from the 12th century which have been interpreted as being a **"stofa"**, a substantial wooden farmhouse, so far unique in Shetland. That the Norse house was buried beneath a later one was probably why it was preserved and perhaps confirms the suspicions that Norse houses are

Aerial view of Papa Stour from the west - Fogla and Lyra Skerries in the foreground

rare in Shetland because they have been built over.

Shetland had been ruled directly from Norway since 1195 with taxes being raised through the King's representative or *"syssel-man"*. Interestingly the oldest Shetland-related document dates from 1299 and describes a meeting at a *"stofa"* on *"Papey"* to resolve a dispute between Ragnhild Simumunsdatter, who owned land on Papa Stour and Duke Thorvald Thoresson, who was *sysselman* at the time.

Thorvald held a substantial amount of power in Shetland and was accused of illegally raising the taxation due by *udallers* on Papa Stour. The matter was put before the *Ting* and then the King but the outcome is unknown. What is most interesting is the light thrown on the role of women and democracy in 1299.

There are several fine beaches on the island, notably those at Kirk Sand, Housa Voe and at the head of Robie's Noust which make a fine contrast to the rugged cliffs.

Geordie Peterson and grandson making hay coles

The **VE SKERRIES** (ON *Westsker* - West Skerries) lie about 3 miles north west of Papa Stour and have claimed the crews of many wrecked ships. The low-lying and rounded gneiss rocks may look innocuous on a summer's day but cannot be easily seen in breaking seas.

Perhaps the most prominent loss was when the Aberdeen trawler ***Ben Doran*** ran onto the Ve Skerries in March 1930 during a severe gale. Despite the efforts of several boats, including the Stromness lifeboat from Orkney which arrived to find the trawler gone, all of the crew were lost. As a result the **Aith Lifeboat Station** was established in 1933.

A small lighthouse now marks

the danger. It was constructed in 1979, the lamphouse being reused from the North Carr lightship. In autumn the Ve Skerries are host to one of Shetlands largest Grey Seal colonies when the seals haul out to pup and mate.

Shetland Museum
Ve Skerries lighthouse

Kirstan Hole is one of the largest caves on Papa Stour
Shetland Museum

Ve Skerries
Shetland Museum

FOULA

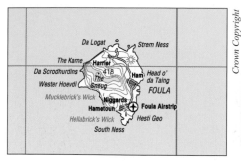

Crown Copyright

Foula - aerial view from the south with The Kame (376m), T

FOULA (ON *Fugla-ey* - Bird Isle, or perhaps *Ytra-ey* - Outer Isle) is the remotest inhabited island in the UK. It is only 3 miles long, with an area of about 1265ha, but the maximum height of 418m makes it feel larger.

Most of the island is composed of Old Red Sandstone

which forms the dramatic western cliffs, while the low-lying north east is ancient gneiss and schist. The coast is almost totally rockbound, with only one small beach at **Ham Voe**, near the pier.

The harbour is so exposed that the ferry *New Advance*

has to be lifted out of the water when not in use. A trip to Foula may easily be cancelled by rough seas or fog, but is very much worth the effort, whether by air for a day trip or sea for a longer visit.

Although the island bears some superficial comparison with St Kilda, the Foula men have always been fishermen who also cultivated the land and harvested the huge numbers of breeding seabirds. By contrast the St Kildans were neither fishermen nor crofters.

Along with North Ronaldsay in Orkney, Foula was the last bastion of the *Norn* language, which was spoken until the late 18th century. The island also still celebrates *"Old Yule"*, using the Julian rather than the Gregorian calendar, introduced in 1753. The Foula folk thus celebrate Christmas on 6th January and New Year's Day on 13th January.

The west cliffs of Foula rate with those of St Kilda and

Shetland Museum

The "Oceanic" ran ashore on the Da Shaalds O'Foula in 1914

Soberlie Hill and the North Bank

...m) and The Noup (248m)

Gaada Stack off the north coast is perforated by a natural arch

Hoy in Orkney as the highest and most spectacular in Britain. In the breeding season they are home to many thousands of nesting seabirds, attracted by the rich feeding grounds surrounding the island.

Foula backlit by a winter sunset, seen from Eshaness

On a clear day a climb to the highest point of the island, **The Sneug** (ON *Knjukr* - conical, steep hill, 418m) will give a panoramic view of the whole of the west of Shetland and the hilltops of Orkney to the south. Of the off-lying stacks perhaps **Gaada Stack** in the north with its natural arch is the most spectacular, but pride of place must go to the **The Kame** with its near-vertical 376m cliff.

Traditional hay-making at Ham

Today over 3,000 Great Skuas, or Bonxies, nest on the island. This is a major recovery from the 3 pairs nesting in 1920, after much 19th century persecution. The island also has its own subspecies of field mouse.

A day trip to Foula involves a choice - strenuous hike to the top of the hill to see the cliffs, or a gentler walk to the north end. Both will beckon a return.

The small harbour at Ham Voe on the east side

Lighthouse at the South Ness

157

FAIR ISLE

"Shaalder" at the North Haven before the breakwater was built

FAIR ISLE (ON *Fridarey* - Truce Isle) lies midway between Sumburgh Head and North Ronaldsay in Orkney. Although only 3 miles long, it has much to interest the visitor.

The island is composed of Old Red Sandstone which weathers to produce fertile soils, and erodes to form dramatic cliffs which exceed 170m below the **Ward Hill** (HZ208734, 217m). Most of the coastline is rock-bound apart from the North Haven with its sandy beach and the South Haven which has a shingle beach. There are also small beaches at the South Harbour.

Despite the building of a break-water and new pier, the exposed situation means that the ferry, ***Good Shepherd***, is hauled out of the water between trips except in very fair weather. The 2.5 hour trip from Grutness, near Sumburgh, is an adventure in itself, and offers good opportunities to see cetaceans and seabirds, although many feed the fish instead!

The island became famous in the early 20th century for pioneering studies on bird migration, and the **Bird Observatory** established in 1948 by George Waterston remains a very important part of its economy.

The island is well situated for such studies as it lies on the main migration routes from Iceland, Greenland and Scandanavia to Britain. At least 359 species have been observed on Fair Isle, of which about 45 are regular breeders. Of over 320,000 birds which have been ringed and released nearly 5,000 have sub-sequently been "controlled".

Due to its small size and relative-ly low cliffs, Fair Isle is a good place to view most of the com-mon breeding seabirds and waders. Those wishing to see Puffins close-to will not be dis-appointed. The island has its own sub-species of Wren and Fieldmouse. The former will

The North Haven from the west with "Good Shepherd" moored alongside

The headland of Skroo is the site of the North Light

soon make its presence clear, while the latter is understandably more discrete.

There are about 250 species of flowering plants on Fair Isle. During a good summer the whole island becomes awash with a sea of colours - blues, reds, yellows - as the various species flower. The relatively low sheep density compared to most of Shetland greatly helps. Most of the north of the island is maritime heath or heather moorland, in contrast to the croftlands of the south end.

Although there are no large intact "ancient monuments" there are many archaeological sites, including prehistoric houses, cairns and field systems which emerge from the peat at the north end. The landscape is also dotted with many burnt mounds, including the largest in Shetland at **Houlalie** above Punds (HZ203716). The *"Feelie Dyke"* (turf dyke) separates the hill to the north from the southern fields, and is undoubtedly ancient. The 19th century hill dyke parallels it.

No brochs have been found on Fair Isle, but there is a small promontory fort called **Landberg** (HZ223723) overlooking the isthmus between the North and South Havens. With ramparts and evidence of buildings this enigmatic site awaits

further investigation. Pottery fragments found here suggest a late Iron Age date.

So far no Norse structure has been identified on Fair Isle, but the Vikings have certainly left their mark in the place and farm

The North Light

"Good Shepherd" on her slipway

Ian Best, traditional boatbuilder, at work

FAIR ISLE

Fair Isle South Light and South Harbour from the east

names as elsewhere in the Northern Isles. Although there is no physical evidence for early Norse settlement *Fridarey* gets several mentions in the sagas. There was a warning beacon which could be lit on **Malcolm's Head**, later the site of a wartime lookout.

Due to its position in the middle of the northabout shipping route between Orkney and Shetland, Fair Isle was a graveyard for many sailing ships, due to fog, darkness, storms or just bad navigation in attempting to avoid the dangerous Sumburgh Roost or low-lying North Ronaldsay with its strong tides.

The south end from above Springfield

Perhaps the most famous shipwreck was the *El Gran Grifon*, a chartered supply ship from Rostock, which had taken part in the Spanish Armada, and which was driven ashore at Stroms Heliar on 28th September 1588. Nearly 300 crew and soldiers survived, but about 50 died of starvation before they were repatriated. An iron cross in the kirkyard commemorates those who died.

The airstrip was built during WWII to service the radar station on the Ward Hill. After over 60 years the hastily constructed and partially demolished site still awaits tidying up by the British

Government. Other evidence of the war are the remains of a **Heinkel HE111** shot down in 1941 (HZ213716) whilst on a reconnaisance flight.

Stained glass window in the kirk

German aircraft often attacked lighthouses, and in December 1941 the wife of one of the keepers at the South Light was killed. In January 1942 a direct hit on the accommodation block resulted in the death of another keeper's wife and daughter as well as a soldier who was operating an AA gun.

The north and south lighthouses were built in 1892 by the Stevensons, partly to assist the manoeuvres of the Royal Navy, and partly to stem the number of shipwrecks, which however continued well into the 20th century until the advent of electronic navigation aids finally almost stopped ships finding the rocks of Fair Isle. The South Light was the last to be automated in Scotland, in 1998.

Landberg promontory fort

The islanders have long been well known for their intricate and distinctive knitwear. It is not clear when knitting first became a fashion, but certainly it was established well before the Spanish Armada shipwreck. For centuries boats would put out to trade with passing sailing ships, exchanging knitwear for all kinds of commodities. The advent of fast steamships put an end to this.

WWII German Heinkel HE111 tail

The **George Waterston Centre** in the old school is the local heritage museum and well worth a look, as is the nearby kirk with its modern stained glass windows. **Fair Isle Lodge & Bird Observatory** is situated at the North Haven (Tel 01595 760258).

Crofts at the fertile south end

Old yoles in their nousts at the South Harbour

NorthLink ferry "Hjaltland" passing Kirkabister Ness light on Bressay whilst arriving in Lerwick

GETTING TO SHETLAND

Shetland may appear to be isolated and remote, but in fact it has excellent transport links with Scotland by air and sea. There are good connections to all four major Scottish airports, with Aberdeen being only an hour by air. The main ferry link is also with Aberdeen.

AIR Loganair fly into Sumburgh Airport at the south end of Shetland by a variety of routes, from Orkney, Aberdeen, Edinburgh, Glasgow and Inverness. Flights operate seven days per week. For reservations and enquires Tel 01950 460345, check the Loganair website at www.loganair.co.uk or the BA website at www.ba.com.

Atlantic Airways operates a twice weekly service from Sumburgh to Stansted, London from June to September. Tel 020 7823 4242, www.atlantic.fo

SEA NorthLink Ferries operate two large new ferries on the Lerwick to Aberdeen route. The services run overnight in both directions and call at Kirkwall in Orkney several times per week. For information about timetables and reservations call **0845 6000 449**, or check the Northlink website at www.northlinkferries.co.uk

The NorthLink ferries *Hjaltland* and *Hrossey* are 12,000GRT, 125m long and cruise at 24 knots. Lerwick to Aberdeen takes 12 hours, while Lerwick to Kirkwall and Kirkwall to Aberdeen each take 5 hours.

Connections to Scotland via Orkney are provided by Northlink's ferry *Hamnavoe* which runs several times per day from Stromness to Scrabster.

Sumburgh Airport with Fitful Head in the background

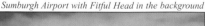

SEA - Scandanavia - the **Smyril Line** vessel *Norrona* links Lerwick to Torshavn in the Faeroes, Seydisfjordur in Iceland, and Hantsholm in Denmark from May to September. The vessel also runs from Bergen to Scrabster and from Scrabster to the Faeroes.

For information and reservations Tel **+298 345900** or check the Smyril Line website at www.smyril-line.com

John Leask & Son in Lerwick are the experts for holidays in Shetland travel, accommodation, car hire and coach tours. Their local knowledge enables them to offer attractive prices and package deals, Tel 01595 693162., www.leaskstravel.co.uk.

GETTING AROUND IN SHETLAND Shetland is much larger than it looks on the small inset maps so favoured by map-makers. As a result visitors should either consider taking their own car, or hiring a car for at least part of their visit so as to allow freedom to reach their favoured sites.

Bolts and **John Leask & Son** are the leading car hire firms locally, and care should be taken to book in advance to avoid disappointment. For those without transport John Leask & Son operate conducted coach tours to the main sites.

VisitShetland will advise about the several local businesses offering minibus or guided tours, boat trips and wildlife tours. Island Trails and Shetland Geotours offer unique experiences which should not be missed.

Shetland is good cycling territory, apart from the wind, and many visitors bring their bikes. Bicycles may be hired in Lerwick. Perhaps the best way to appreciate the Shetland landscape is on foot.

Many walks are suggested in this book, but for further information the visitor is strongly recommended to purchase the relevant Ordnance Survey map(s).

Remember, *"Leave only footsteps, take only memories and photos."*

SHETLAND ISLANDS COUNCIL

Department of Infrastructure Services
20 Commercial Road ZE1 0LX
Tel 01595 744868 Fax 01595 744880

PUBLIC TRANSPORT in Shetland comprises an integrated bus, ferry and air service covering all of the parishes and inhabited islands. Full details are available in the annual *Shetland Transport Timetable,* published by Zetland Transport Partnership, which provides the latest information on all services.

The **latest timetable information** on all local bus, air and ferry services is available by calling **01595 744868** or **01595 744886** (SIC Transport Office).

Viking Bus Station, Lerwick

BUS SERVICES in Shetland are provided by the **Zetland Transport Partnership** and operated by various local companies. There are services covering the Lerwick area, all of the Mainland and the North Isles. Please note that some do not operate in school holidays or on Sundays.

"Islander" at Fair Isle

AIR SERVICES within Shetland are operated from Tingwall Airport near Lerwick to Fair Isle, Out Skerries, Foula and Papa Stour by **Directflight Ltd**, Tel **01595 840246**. All bookings and enquiries should be made to this number. The company flies 8-seat Islander aircraft, which allow easy access to the remoter islands, and give spectacular views along the way.

INTER-ISLAND FERRY SERVICES are operated by Shetland Islands Council to the following islands (except for Foula):

Bressay from Lerwick
     (no bookings)
Yell, Unst and Fetlar from Toft
  (bookings 01957 722259)
Whalsay from Laxo
  (bookings 01806 566259)
Out Skerries from Vidlin
  (bookings 01806 515226)
Papa Stour from West Burrafirth
  (bookings 01957 722259)
Foula from Walls
  (bookings 07881 823732)
Fair Isle from Grutness
  (bookings 01595 760222)

It is advisable to plan and book all ferry crossings, especially at busy times. Bookings can be made or changed during normal office hours. Booking is essential on the crossings to the remoter islands. Visitors should also note that 20 Journey Tickets are available which represent more than a 50% saving when travelling around.

MV "Linga" leaving Laxo

Foula Ferry The Foula to Walls ferry is operated by Atlantic Ferries.Ltd. The service runs twice weekly with an additional sailing in the summer - all however, subject to the current weather and sea conditions. Please call 07881 823732 for up to date sailing information.

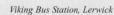

Viking Bus Station, Lerwick

Seafood platter with Lobster

ACCOMMODATION & EATING OUT

Kveldsro House Hotel Greenfield Place, Lerwick, Shetland ZE1 0AQ
Tel 01595 692195
Fax 01595 696595
www.shetlandhotels.com
reception@kveldsrohotel.co.uk
****SMALL HOTEL The country house hotel in the centre of town; attentive 4 star service

Lerwick Hotel , 15 South End Road, Lerwick, Shetland ZE1 0RB
Tel 01595 692166
Fax 01595 694419
www.shetlandhotels.com
reception@lerwickhotel.co.uk
***HOTEL Stunning views over the bay, brasserie restaurant and renowned seafood restaurant

Shetland Hotel, Holmsgarth Road, Lerwick, Shetland ZE1 0PW
Tel 01595 695515
Fax 01595 685828
www.shetlandhotels.com
reception@shetlandhotel.co.uk
*** HOTEL - modern 64 bedroomed hotel conveniently near to ferry terminal, with Beltrami's Cafe/bar and the Oasis restaurant;

NorthLink tickets

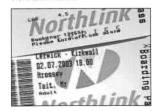

Glen Orchy House, 20 Knab Road, Lerwick ZE1 0AX
Tel/Fax 01595 692031
www.guesthouselerwick.com
STB***GUEST HOUSE, 23 rooms (all en suite), near town centre in quiet part of town.

Spiggie Hotel, Scousburgh, Shetland ZE2 9JE
Tel 01950 460409
Fax 01950 460674
*** SMALL HOTEL 4 rooms (all en suite) A small family-run country hotel situated in a unique location in the South Mainland.

Sumburgh Hotel, Sumburgh, Shetland ZE2 9JN
Tel 01950 460201
Fax 01950 460194
sumburgh-hotel@zetnet.co.uk
www.sumburgh-hotel@zetnet.co.uk
*** HOTEL, 32 rooms (all *en suite*). With true Shetland Character. Superbly situated and ideal for lazy holidays, business visits and meals.

Captain Flint's Lounge Bar & Pool Room, above D&G Leslie, Market Cross, Lerwick. Bar Food served all day.

St Ninian's Cafe and Gallery, Bigton, South Mainland, Shetland Overlooking St Ninian's Isle
Tel 01950 422417

Braewick Cafe and Caravan Park, Eshaness, Shetland ZE2 9RS Spectacular views of the Drongs and St Magnus Bay. Cafe/restaurant, craft shop, gallery, caravan park and camping site
Tel 01806 503345
www.eshaness.shetland.co.uk
braewick@hotmail.co.uk

Da Haaf Restaurant, North Atlantic Fisheries College, Scalloway
Tel 01595 880747
For Quality Shetland Seafood Lunches and Evening Meals. Extensive fish menu, meat and vegetarian dishes also available.

SHOPPING

D&G Leslie, Ellesmere Stores, Market Cross, Lerwick. Fruit & Vegetables, Confectionery, Newsagent, Bakery, Wines & Spirits.

Messrs CG Williamson, Bixter, Shetland
Tel 01595 810200
General Merchants, Off Sales, Crafts, Petrol & Diesel.

"Fair Isle" handknitted jumper

Mainlands Ltd, Dunrossness Industrial Estate, South Mainland
Tel 01950 460676
Fax 01950 460833
General Merchant, Petrol Station, Gifts & Greens, Post Office & Off Licence.
shop@mainlands.co.uk

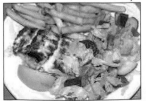

Turbot &chips

KNITWEAR

Shetland Collection, Orcadia, Exnaboe, Virkie, Shetland ZE2 9JS
Tel/Fax 01950 460340
doreen.brown@zetnet.co.uk
www.shetlandknitwear.net
"The Natural Choice" - choose from a fine collection of Shetland Knitwear.

Anderson & Co, The Shetland Warehouse, Lerwick, Shetland ZE1 0BD
Tel 01595 693715
pottingers@aol.com
www.shetlandknitwear.com
Genuine home produced Real Shetland Knitwear & Souvenirs.

Shetland Sirloin

MUSEUMS & VISITOR ATTRACTIONS

Shetland Museum and Archives, Hays Dock, Lerwick, Shetland ZE1 0EL
Tel 01595 695057
Fax 01595 696728
tommy@sic.shetland-museum.or.uk
www.shetland-museum.org.uk
Shetland Museum and Archives, Bod of Gremista, Lerwick, Croft House Museum, Boddam, Dunrossness. On-line photographic archive.

Quendale Water Mill, Dunrossness, South Mainland
Tel 01950460969/01595 859251
www.quendalemill.shetland.co.uk
Restored 19th century over-shot water mill, craft shop, coffees & teas.
Open May to September

TRANSPORT

NorthLink Orkney & Shetland Ferries Ltd, Kiln Corner, Ayre Road, Kirkwall, Orkney KW15 1QX
Reservations Tel 0845 6000 449
Head Office 01856 885500
Fax 01856 879588
info@northlinkferries.co.uk
www.northlinkferries.co.uk
"Here to get you there", NorthLink operates three new ferries on the Lerwick - Kirkwall - Aberdeen and Stromness - Scrabster routes

John Leask & Son, The Esplanade, Lerwick, Shetland ZE1 0LL
Tel 01595 693162
Fax 01595 693171
linfo@leaskstravel.co.uk
www.leaskstravel.co.uk
Travel agents and tour operators - the local experts. Also mini coaches and coaches and self-drive car hire.

Bolts Car Hire, Toll Clock Shopping Centre, 26 North Road, Lerwick, Shetland ZE1 0PE
Tel 01595 693636
Fax 01595 694646
info@boltscarhire.co.uk
www.boltscarhire.co.uk
Shetland's leading rental fleet offers a wide range of modern vehicles for hire.

Shetland Islands Council, Department of Infrastructure Services, 20 Commercial Road, Lerwick, Shetland ZE1 0LX
Tel 01595 744868
Fax 01595 744880
Integrated public transport by bus, ferry and air service covering all of the parishes and inhabited islands. For latest timetable information call 01595 744868 or 01595 744886

"Fair Isle" handknitted jumper

Shetland Halibut

TOURS

Mousa Boat Trips
Mid-April to Mid-September - Booking Essential
Tel 01950 431367
Mobile 07901 872339
www.mousaboattrips.co.uk
Visits to Mousa Broch

Island Trails by Elma Johnston. The warmest of welcomes to Shetland, storytelling, tours - landscape, history and people.
Tel 01950 422408
Fax 01950 422255
www.island-trails.co.uk
info@island-trails.co.uk

Shetland Geotours for the Shetland experience, geology, archaeology, wildlife, scenic tours and guided walks
Tel 01595 859218
info@shetlandgeology.com
www.shetlandgeology.com

PHOTOGRAPHY

Charles Tait Photographic Ltd, Kelton, St Ola, Orkney KW15 1TR
Tel 01856 873738
Fax 01856 875313
charles.tait@zetnet.co.uk
www.charles-tait.co.uk
Photographers and Publishers,. Photo Library Shetland, Orkney , Western Isles and Northern Scotland. Natural History, Landscapes, Archaeology, History Large selection of Shetland images and other available to view online.

During the research for this book several hundred books, periodicals, guides, maps and other publications were consulted as well as many individuals and websites. The author wishes to thank everyone who has been of assistance during his years of wanderings in Shetland, as well as those who did the essential jobs of proof-reading and image correction.

The following bibliography is a distillation of many of the books on the area. Some are essential reading, while others depend on personal interests. Sea-lovers may find Hamish Haswell-Smith's book on the Scottish Islands a good starting place.

Many locally-produced leaflets, guides and small books are available produced by the Tourist Board, Scottish Natural H and other bodies or indivi Apart from the Shetland T Bookshop in Lerwick, m shops throughout the isles st local books. The Tourist Boar visitor attractions, heritage centre and museums are also goo sources of local publications, some of which are free, while others may be charged for.

ESSENTIAL BACKGROUND READING

The Scottish Islands	Hamish Haswell-Smith	Canongate	1996
Bobby Tulloch's Shetland	Bobby Tulloch	Macmillan	1988
A Naturalist's Shetland	J Laughton Johnston	T&AD Poyser	1999

GUIDE BOOKS

Shetland	Jill Slee Blackadder	Colin Baxter Photography	2003
Shetland	Anna Ritchie	The Stationery Office	1997
A Guide to Prehistoric and Viking Shetland	Noel Fojut	Shetland Times	1993
Shetland, An illustrated Architectural Guide	Mike Finnie	Mainstream	1990

GENERAL BOOKS ON SHETLAND

Shetland in Statistics 2001	Development Department	Shetland Islands Council	2001
Orkney & Shetland - Geology	W Mykura	HMSO	1976
The Orkneys and Shetland	John R Tudor	Edward Stanford	1883
Orkney & Schetland 1774	George Low	Melven Press	1879
The Shetland Story	Liv K Schei & Gunni Moberg	Batsford	1988
The Northern Isles: Orkney & Shetland	Alexander Fenton	John Donald	1978

ARCHAEOLOGY & HISTORY

Old Scatness Broch Field season 2002	SJ Dockrill, JM Bond & VE Turner	Shetland Amenity Trust	2003
Jarlshof A Walk Through the Past	Patrick Ashmore	Historic Scotland	2002
Ancient Shetland	Val Turner	BT Batsford	1998
Fair Isle The Archaeology of an Island Community	JR Hunter	HMSO	1996
The Brochs of Mousa and Clickimin	John Hamilton	HMSO	1983
The Biggings Papa Stour	Barbara E Crawford & Beverly B Smith	Soc of Antiqu of Scotland	1999
Papa Stour and 1299	ed Barbara E Crawford	Shetland Times	2002
Scord of Brouster	Alasdair Whittle et al	Oxford University	1986
Pytheas the Greek	Barry Cunliffe	Penguin Press	2001

VIKING PERIOD

The Papar in the North Atlantic	ed Barbara E Crawford	University of St Andrews	2002
Westward Before Columbus	Kore Prytz	Norsk Maritim Forlag	1991
The N and W Isles in the Viking World	ed A Fenton & H Palsson	John Donald	1984
Orkneyinga Saga	trans. H P Isson & P Edwards	Hogarth	1978

HISTORY-SCOTTISH CONNECTION

Black Patie - Patrick Stewart	Peter Anderson	John Donald	1992
The Ice-Bound Whalers	ed James A Troup	Orkney Press	1987
Toons and Tenants	Brian Smith	Shetland Times	2000
Shetland Documents 1195-1579	JH Ballantyne & Brian Smith	Shetland Times	1999
Shetland and the Outside World 1469-1969	ed Donald J Withrington	Aberdeen Univ Press	1983

LANGUAGE AND CULTURE

The Norn Language of Orkney and Shetland	Michael P Barnes	Shetland Times	1998
Shetland Place-names	John Stewart	Shet Library &Museum	1987
The Shetland Dictionary	John J Graham	Shetland Times	1993
Shetland's Northern Links, Language & History	ed Doreen J Waugh	Scot Soc Northern Studies	1996
Grammar and Usage of the Shetland Dialect	TA Robertson & JJ Graham	Shetland Times	1952

WALKS

Walking the Coastline of Shetland 1 - Yell	Peter Guy	Shetland Times	1996
Walking the Coastline of Shetland 2 - Unst	Peter Guy	Unst Heritage Centre	1990
Walking the Coastline of Shetland 3 - Fetlar	Peter Guy	Sullom Voe Scene Publ	1991
Walking the Coastline of Shetland 4 - Northmavine	Peter Guy	Sullom Voe Scene Publ	1992
Walking the Coastline of Shetland 5 - Westside	Peter Guy	Shetland Times	1995
Walking the Coastline of Shetland 6 - South Mainland	Peter Guy	Shetland Times	2000

NATURAL HISTORY

Scottish Birds, Culture and Tradition	Robin Hull	Mercat Press	2001
Shetland's Wild Flowers	D Malcolm	Shetland Times	1990
Rare Plants of Shetland	Scott, Harvey, Riddington & Fisher	Shetland Amenity Trust	2002
Plants & People in Ancient Scotland	Camilla Dickson & James Dickson	Tempus	2000
Where to Watch Birds in Shetland	Hugh Harrop	Hugh Harrop	2000
Guide to Whales, Dolphins & Porpoises	Peter GH Evans	Seawatch Foundation	1995
A Guide to Shetland's Breeding Birds	Bobby Tulloch	Shetland Times	1992
Shetland Bird Report	ed Mike Pennington	Shetland Bird Club	2001
The Birds of Fair Isle	JN Dymond		1991
Fair Isle Bird Observatory Report 2000	ed Deryk and Hollie Shaw	FIBO	2001

SEA AND BOATS

In Da Galley	Charlie Simpson	Shetland Times	2000
The Swan, Shetland's legacy of Sail	James R Nicholson	Shetland Times	1999
Orkney and Shetland Steamers	Alistair Deayton	Tempus	2002
Shetland Fishermen	James R Nicholson	Shetland Times	1999
The Saga of the Earls	Adam Robson	Shetland Times	2002
The Sail Fishermen of Shetland	A Halcrow	Shetland Times	1994
Shipwrecks of Orkney & Shetland	David M Ferguson	David & Charles	1988
Scotland's Northern Lights	Sharma Krauskopf	Shetland Times	2003

CULTURE, TRADITION

Shetland Dye Book	Jenni Simmons	Shetland Times	1985
Knitting by the Fireside and on the Hillside	Linda G Fryer	Shetland Times	1995
A Century of Shetlands	ed Angela Gosling	Shetl Pony Stud-Book Soc	1987
Guidebook to the Croft House Museum	Ian Tait	Shetland Museum	2000
Up Helly Aa	Callum G Brown	Mandolin	1998
Go Listen to the Crofters	AD Cameron	Acair	1986
Shetland Breeds	ed Nancy Kohlberg & Philip Kopper	Posterity Press	2003
Shetland Wool	Stanley Bowie	Shetland Publishing Co	1997
Shetland Sheep	Stanley Bowie	The Abbey Press	1998

20th CENTURY

Airfield Focus 13: Sullom Voe & Scatsta	Peter Ward	GMS Enterprises	1994
A History of Scatsta Airfield, Shetland	Terry Mayes	Prosper Comms	2001
The Giving Years, 1939-1945	James W Irvine	Shetland Publishing Co	1991
The Shetland Bus	David Howarth	Shetland Times	1998
Shetland Bus Faces and Places 60 years on	Trygve Sorvaag	Shetland Times	2002
Island Challenge	Edward Thomason	Shetland Times	1997
In a World O'Wir Ane	Susan Telford	Shetland Times	1998
A Vehement Thirst After Knowledge	John J Graham	Shetland Times	1998

PHOTOGRAPH BOOKS

Shetland, Land of the Ocean	Colin Baxter & Jim Crumley	Colin Baxter Photography	1992
Shetland, Terre de Vent	Georges Dif	Milan	1989

STORIES AND FOLKLORE

Shetland Folk-Lore	John Spence	Johnson & Greig, Lerwick	1899
The Folklore of Orkney & Shetland	Ernest W Marwick	Batsford	1975

MAPS

Shetland is covered by Ordnance Survey Landranger1:50,000 sheets 1-4 and by Explorer 1:25,000 sheets 466-470

INDEX

The Gateway for Shetland's Heritage and Culture

museum
Shetland
archives

Shetland's story starts here ....

LK637

Shetland Museum and Archives,
Hay's Dock, Lerwick, ZE1 0WP
www.shetlandmuseumandarchives.org.uk
T: +44 (0)1595 695057